JLA

NOTES

including

- *Life of the Author*
- *General Plot Summary*
- *List of Characters*
- *Summaries & Critical Commentaries*
- *German Expressionism and the American Horror Film*
- *Selected Filmography*
- *Topics for Discussion*
- *Selected Bibliography*

by
Samuel J. Umland, Ph.D.
Department of English
University of Nebraska

Editor

Gary Carey, M.A.
University of Colorado

Consulting Editor

James L. Roberts, Ph.D.
Department of English
University of Nebraska

ISBN 0-8220-0417-8

Printed in U.S.A.

1995 Printing

Cliffs Notes, Inc. Lincoln, Nebraska

CONTENTS

DRACULA NOTES

LIFE OF THE AUTHOR

Many of the events of Bram Stoker's life are still a mystery and are open to speculation. Most biographers have had to rely on public records to determine the interests and life of the author, thus prompting Daniel Farson, Stoker's grandnephew and also one of his biographers, to write: "Stoker has long remained one of the least known authors of one of the best-known books ever written."

We know that Bram Stoker was born in Dublin, Ireland, on November 8, 1847, the third son of seven children. Sickly and bedridden as a child, Stoker eventually grew to well over six feet in height and became athletic and muscular, crowned with a head of thick, red hair. He is referred to by biographer Farson as a "red-haired giant." As a student at Trinity College in Dublin, Stoker graduated with honors in science, and he later returned to the college for an M.A. degree.

It appears that Stoker was always interested in writing because, for a time, he worked as a drama critic; additionally, the author whom he most admired was Walt Whitman, whose controversial book of poetry, *Leaves of Grass*, Stoker publicly defended. After years of correspondence, Stoker finally met Whitman in 1884, and he met him again a few more times, the last time in 1887. Stoker also worked for the Irish civil service, much like his father had done.

In 1876, when Stoker was twenty-nine years old, he met the famous and talented actor Henry Irving, a meeting which became of great value to both men. Of course, Stoker had seen Irving many times before this, witnessing with awe Irving's considerable dramatic talent. Stoker and Irving became close friends, and Stoker soon became the actor-manager of Irving's theater. Stoker appears to have enjoyed the life of the theater for he held the position for twenty-seven years, beginning in 1878, until Irving's death in October of 1905.

In 1878, Stoker married Florence Balcombe, who had had the choice of marrying either Bram Stoker or Oscar Wilde. At the time, Stoker was thirty-one years old, Wilde only twenty-four. Stoker and Wilde remained friends, however, and Stoker was admitted into Wilde's literary circle. During his life Bram Stoker met many leading artistic and prominent figures of his day; in addition to Oscar Wilde, he entertained Arthur Conan Doyle, Alfred Lord Tennyson, Mark Twain, and once he even met Theodore Roosevelt. Bram Stoker's son and only child, Noel, was born in 1879, and in 1882 Stoker published his first substantial literary effort, *Under the Sunset,* a collection of tales for children.

Evidently, Stoker was a man of considerable energy and talent. As well as being acting manager of Irving's theater, he delivered lectures, traveled extensively, toured with Irving's acting company, and he wrote several novels, as well as several works of non-fiction. His first novel, a romance entitled *The Snake's Pass,* was published in 1890. Then, written over a period of several years, beginning in 1890, Stoker's masterpiece, *Dracula,* was published by Archibald Constable in 1897. The book has continued to grip the public's imagination ever since, and it has never been out of print since its publication. Upon the publication of *Dracula,* Charlotte Stoker, the author's mother, felt the book would bring Bram immediate success, and she personally liked the book very much.

Stoker dedicated *Dracula* to one of his close friends, Hall Caine, who was also a novelist; in fact, few people know that the "dear friend Hommy-Beg" of the dedication is Hall Caine. "Hommy-Beg" is an affectionate childhood nickname for Caine, which means "little Tommy."

During his recovery from a stroke which occurred soon after Irving's death, Stoker wrote a book of non-fiction which he called *Personal Reminiscences of Henry Irving* (1906), a volume about both the famous English actor and Stoker himself. Meanwhile, Stoker had earlier published *The Mystery of the Sea,* in 1902, and he produced another romantic novel, *The Man,* in 1905. Both novels are interesting reading, primarily for their examination of the roles of women in society, as well as for Stoker's characterization of women.

Stoker did not cease to write stories of horror and mystery after he finished *Dracula.* After *Dracula,* his novels of mystery and horror include *The Jewel of Seven Stars* (1903), a compelling Rider Haggard-like tale of adventure and romance set in Egypt, *The Lady of the*

Shroud (1909), and *The Lair of the White Worm* (1911), both of which are interesting novels and deserve more than a passing glance, though they are not near the achievement that *Dracula* is. Some of Stoker's short tales of horror, particularly "Dracula's Guest," an episode cut from the final version of *Dracula*, as well as the Poe-like "The Judge's House," are very good and well worth reading.

Regardless of which novel Stoker himself considered his best, *Dracula* remains his most popular work, and it has spawned countless adaptations and spin-offs in plays, novels, and movies, as well as comic books. Critical analyses and psychological interpretations of *Dracula* abound.

In his last years, Stoker's health declined rapidly, and the cause of his death, though clouded by mystery, has generated some substantial amount of discussion. His biographers have been reticent to discuss it. Recently, though, Daniel Farson, Stoker's grandnephew, in his biography, cites Stoker's death certificate, which has as the cause of death the medical phrase *Locomotor Ataxy*—also called *Tabes Dorsalis*—known in those days as general paralysis of the insane, which implies, therefore, that Stoker had contracted syphilis, presumably around the turn of the century, and died of it. If Stoker died of syphilis, it will probably remain only speculation, since the truth of the matter hinges on whether or not *Locomotor Ataxy* can be construed as being syphilis.

Stoker's literary efforts certainly hold some degree of achievement, and these efforts probably represent those things by which he should be remembered. Stoker died on April 20, 1912, at the age of sixty-four.

GENERAL PLOT SUMMARY

Sometime in the late nineteenth century, Jonathan Harker, a young English lawyer, is traveling to the Castle Dracula, which is located in Transylvania, in order to finalize a transfer of real estate in England to Count Dracula. Harker becomes extremely nervous when all of the local peasants react in fear after they hear of his destination; nevertheless, he continues on to the castle until he meets an emissary of the Count in the Borgo Pass. The mysterious coach driver continues on to the castle, arriving in pitch darkness, to the accompaniment of howling wolves.

Even though his accomodations are comfortable, Harker finds Count Dracula to be a pale, gaunt, thin man, rather strange, and Harker is mortified when, after accidentally cutting himself shaving, the Count lunges at Harker's throat in "demoniac fury." Harker soon finds himself imprisoned within the castle and assailed by three seductive female vampires, whom he can barely stave off. Harker also discovers the Count's secret – that is, the Count survives by drinking the blood of human beings – and, now, he is intent on killing Harker. The Count escapes Jonathan's attempt to kill him, and he swiftly leaves the castle with fifty boxes of earth, bound for England. The last we hear of Jonathan Harker, he is weak and sick, left alone with no visible means of escape from the castle.

The novel then shifts to England, where Harker's fiancée, Mina Murray, is visiting her friend Lucy Westenra, who has accepted the marriage proposal of Arthur Holmwood, while rejecting the proposals of Dr. John Seward, head of a lunatic asylum, and Quincey Morris, an American from Texas, currently visiting Holmwood. Mina's two main concerns are that Lucy has taken up her old habit of sleepwalking, and that it is a long time since she has heard from her own fiancé, Jonathan.

One night while the two women are out walking, they witness the approach of a strange ship. When the ship is wrecked on the beach, the only creature which survives is a huge dog, which quickly disappears. We soon discover that the wrecked ship is carrying fifty boxes of earth from the Castle Dracula.

Soon after the shipwreck, late one night, Mina discovers that Lucy is sleepwalking again. In her search, Mina discovers Lucy on the ladies' favorite seat, near the graveyard overlooking the town. Mina is shocked to see hovering over Lucy a tall, thin, black shape, but when she arrives at Lucy's side the shape has disappeared. When awakened, Lucy remembers nothing of what has happened, except that she is chilled. In wrapping Lucy against the cold, Mina assumes that she inadvertently pricked Lucy with a pin, for she sees two tiny red marks on Lucy's neck. On later, successive nights, Lucy is often found standing at the women's bedroom window; next to her is a creature which appears to be a large bird, but it is, in fact, a bat. Lucy's health declines over the next few weeks, and because of this Mina refuses to tell Lucy about Lucy's mother's sickness. Meanwhile, Dr. Seward, Lucy's former suitor, is unable to ascertain the cause of Lucy's decline.

Soon, Mina hears from Jonathan, and so she leaves Lucy and goes to nurse him. Almost immediately, Lucy's condition deteriorates, and Dr. Seward finds it necessary to wire for his old friend and mentor, Dr. Abraham Van Helsing, who offers another medical opinion. Van Helsing is particularly disturbed by the two tiny spots on Lucy's throat and her apparent but unexplainable loss of blood since there are no signs of hemorrhage.

It becomes necessary to give Lucy numerous blood transfusions, and after each one she improves significantly, only to deteriorate quickly in the next couple of days. Van Helsing finally deems it necessary to drape Lucy's room, as well as her neck, with garlic, a technique, we learn later, which is used to ward off vampires. Eventually, however, the vampire manages to evade the spells against him, and he attacks Lucy again. One significant night, an escaped wolf is used to smash the window of Lucy's room. The wolf's attack so frightens Lucy's mother that she dies of shock, and Lucy, left helpless, is again attacked by the vampire.

Van Helsing, knowing that Lucy is near death, summons her fiancé, Arthur Holmwood, to her side. Holmwood himself comes from the deathbed of his father. As Holmwood bends to kiss Lucy goodbye, Lucy, whose canine teeth have become strangely lengthened, attempts to attack Arthur. As Van Helsing throws Arthur back from her, Lucy dies.

After Lucy's death, the papers report the strange appearance of a person whom the village children label as "the Bloofer Lady," a creature who has been attacking young children in the area. Van Helsing, shaken by the reports, summons Dr. Seward to attend him in an examination of Lucy's coffin. After Seward's initial shock, he agrees, albeit with reservations, to open Lucy's coffin.

In the meantime, Mina and Jonathan have been married, and they return to England. Mina has transcribed Jonathan's diary of his journey in Transylvania, and soon afterward Van Helsing reads it. Van Helsing then calls all of Lucy's ex-suitors together, and he explains to them his belief that Lucy has been bitten by a vampire and has become one herself. The only way to save her soul, he says, is to drive a wooden stake through her heart, cut off her head and stuff it with garlic. Eventually Van Helsing convinces them of the truth of his claims, and the "service" is performed on Lucy.

Now the protagonists begin a search for the Count and also for the fifty boxes of earth which he brought with him to England; these six people–Jonathan, Mina, Dr. Seward, Van Helsing, Holmwood, and Quincey Morris–vow to confront the vampire. Soon after the search begins, Van Helsing realizes that a dreadful change is taking place in Mina. One horrific night, Van Helsing and Seward break into Mina's room, find Jonathan unconscious, and Mina being forced to suck blood from a deep slash across Dracula's chest. In a twinkling, Dracula disappears.

They finally discover and destroy all of the fifty boxes except one, which they learn has been sent by ship back to Dracula's castle. Using various methods, including the hypnosis of Mina, they follow Dracula all the way to the Borgo Pass in Transylvania, where they find the last remaining box being transported to Castle Dracula by a group of gypsies. They overcome the gypsies, throw the box to the ground, tear open its lid, and discover the body of the Count. With a huge thrust, Jonathan cuts off the vampire's head, while Morris drives his knife into the Count's heart. The Count himself crumbles into dust, and Quincey Morris, having been wounded by the gypsies in an attempt to retrieve the box, dies of a mortal wound, and so the novel ends.

LIST OF CHARACTERS

Dracula

He is the vampire who has been "Un-Dead" for several hundred years and keeps his vitality by sucking blood from live victims. He is the Transylvanian Count for whom the book is named. Despite the fact that he is actually seen on only a few of the approximately four hundred pages of the novel, his presence constantly pervades the entire work; of note is the fact that his desire to move from the barren and desolate Transylvania, which is sparsely populated, to the more populous England, is the initiating point of the novel since someone from England must make the trip to Castle Dracula to complete the transactions. In appearance, Count Dracula is described as being a "tall old man, clean shaven, save for a long white mustache and clad in black from head to foot, without a single speck of color about him anywhere." Contrary to popular understanding, Stoker has his Dracula sporting a large, bushy Victorian mustache and having a profuse head of dense, curly hair, massive eyebrows, and peculiarly sharp white teeth, especially the canine teeth. Dracula also possesses astonishing vitality, as is witnessed every time that he appears in a difficult situation.

Jonathan Harker

The young London solicitor who is sent to Transylvania to finalize the transfer of real estate in England to Count Dracula. His journals record the essential facts of his journey from Bistritz to the Borgo Pass, where he is met by Count Dracula's carriage, as well as recording the facts of his arrival and stay at the Castle Dracula. Harker is engaged to a young schoolmistress named Mina Murray.

Miss Mina (Wilhelmina) Murray

The fiancée of Jonathan Harker; she will become a "persecuted maiden" during the latter part of the story. She is quite young, and her job is that of an assistant schoolmistress. She is also an orphan. She will later become Mina Harker and will assist in tracking down Count Dracula.

Miss Lucy Westenra

Mina Murray's closest friend. She is a young woman of nineteen who becomes engaged to Arthur Holmwood. Her penchant for sleepwalking allows her to become Dracula's first victim, and after her "death," she will become one of the "Un-Dead."

Mrs. Westenra

Lucy's mother, who is dying of a heart ailment; she becomes another victim of the vampire.

Arthur Holmwood

A vigorous man, twenty-nine years old, the only son of Lord Godalming; Holmwood will later inherit this title after the death of his father. His engagement to Lucy and the necessity of driving a stake through Lucy's heart after she is one of the "Un-Dead" motivates Holmwood to join in tracking down and exterminating Dracula.

Dr. John Seward

The head of a lunatic asylum, Seward is roughly the same age as Holmwood and is one of Lucy Westenra's suitors. He is an intelligent and determined man.

Quincey P. Morris

Another of Lucy's suitors. Morris is an American from Texas. His great wealth allows him to pay many of the expenses incurred in tracking down Dracula.

Dr. Abraham Van Helsing

An M.D., a Ph.D., and a D.Litt., as well as an attorney. He is a lonely, unmarried old bachelor who is both kindly and fatherly. He is from Amsterdam, and his profound knowledge of medicine, folklore, and the occult allows him to take complete charge of Lucy's illness, which he identifies immediately as vampirism. He is also chiefly in charge of the strategy of tracking down Count Dracula.

R. M. Renfield

A huge, lumbering, fifty-nine-year-old madman who is a patient of Dr. Seward; he also comes under the influence of Dracula.

Mr. Swales

An old man who befriends Lucy and Mina at Whitby, site of the landing of Count Dracula's ship. He is an archetypal figure, the one person who senses and articulates the approaching horror of Dracula, but, Cassandra-like, he is not believed.

CRITICAL COMMENTARIES

CHAPTER 1

Summary

This novel is not told in a straightforward, chronological, omniscient manner, like many nineteenth-century novels. Instead, it is composed of a collage of letters, journal entries and diary jottings, in addition to a portion of a ship's log, various newspaper clippings, and even a "phonograph diary." Since the story is basically a mystery, this technique is highly effective in sustaining suspense, for there are literally dozens of narrative pieces for readers to fit together before they can see the complexity of the novel resolved and the entirety of Stoker's pattern. Stoker most likely borrowed this approach to his novel from Wilkie Collins, who used the same technique in his "detective" novel *The Woman in White* (1860).

Jonathan Harker's journal entries begin on May 3, sometime in the late nineteenth century. The young London lawyer has been traveling by train across Europe and is currently in Budapest, in route to Count Dracula's estate, located somewhere in the Carpathian Mountains of Transylvania – the "land beyond the forest." Harker has been sent by his London law firm to complete the final transactions for a transfer of real estate, which the Count has recently purchased in England, and thus far, Harker is very pleased with his trip. He is favorably impressed with Budapest, and he remarks that already he can tell that he is leaving the Western world behind him and that he is "entering the East," a section of Europe whose peoples and customs will be, for the most part, strange and unfamiliar.

At the beginning of his journey, the tenor of his narrative is low-key – that is, Harker records what he contemplates, what he sees, and what he eats (in regard to the latter, he jots off a couple of reminders to himself to obtain certain recipes for his fiancée, Mina Murray).

As his journal entries continue, Harker continues to record the details of the exotically spiced meals which he dines on, plus descriptions of the many old castles which he sees perched atop steep hills in the distance. The train dawdles on through the countryside, and Harker continues to describe the colorfully costumed peasants whom he sees; he is especially fascinated by the local garb of the swarthy, rather fierce looking men of the region, for they remind him of bandits, but he says that he has been assured that they are quite harmless.

At the eve of twilight, when Harker's train reaches Bistritz, not far from the infamous Borgo Pass, Harker disembarks and checks into the "delightful . . . old fashioned" Golden Krone Hotel (Count Dracula has instructed him to stay here). Before retiring for the night, Harker reads a note of cordial welcome from Count Dracula, then he records some of the local stories about the Pass, as well as some of the other local beliefs and superstitions. For example, the Borgo Pass marks the entry into Bukovina, and the Pass itself has been the scene of great fires and centuries of massacres, famine, and disease. Coincidentally, Harker's arrival at Bistritz is on the eve of St. George's Day, a night when "evil things in the world . . . have full sway." At first, Harker is unconcerned about these local superstitions, but after he witnesses an old peasant woman's fearful awe of the name "Dracula," and after he realizes the extent of her fear for his safety, and after he finally accepts her gift of a rosary to ward off evil spirits, Harker begins to become a bit uneasy about setting off the next day for the Borgo Pass, despite the fact that Dracula's carriage will be waiting for him when he arrives late on the eve of St. George's Day.

The morning of the departure does not bode well: a considerable crowd of peasants has gathered around the coach, muttering polyglot words which all seem to be variants of the word *vampire*; then, almost as if it happens en mass, the crowd makes the sign of the cross and points two fingers at him (a superstitious sign of blessing for a good, safe journey). The coach is off, and in contrast to the rugged road and the feverish haste of the horses, the countryside seems happy, bright, and colorful. But the forest trail, Harker notes, begins to rise ever upward, and soon they begin ascending the lofty, steep terrain of the Carpathian Mountains. The country peasants, as the coach dashes by them, all kneel and cross themselves, and Harker notes that the hills soon pass into a misty and cold gloom. Evening arrives, and soon they are passing beneath ghost-like clouds, as the coach careens alongside late-lying snows. Harker asks to walk, but his request is denied; foot travel is impossible because of the large number of fierce wild dogs in the woods. Meanwhile, the driver lashes his horses onward at an ever faster and more furious speed until at last the coach enters the Borgo Pass.

The passengers disembark, the horses neigh and snort violently, and the peasants suddenly begin screaming. Simultaneously, a horse-drawn caleche drives up, and the driver instructs Harker that he will take him to Count Dracula. Once inside the caleche, Harker collapses in the close darkness, feeling like a child, cowering within the eerie loneliness. Glancing at his watch, he notices in alarm that it is midnight. A wild howling commences, the horses strain and rear, and wolves begin to gather from all sides as fine, powdery snow begins to fall. Harker falls asleep, probably from psychological strain and also from physical weariness; when he awakens, the caleche is stopped and the driver is gone. A ring of wolves "with white teeth and lolling red tongues" surrounds Harker. He feels "a sort of paralysis of fear." The ring of terror is unbearable; he shouts and beats on the side of the caleche. There seems to be no one around. Then without warning, the driver reappears, signals the wolves to disperse, and he drives onward, ascending again, ever higher, until at last they are in the courtyard of a vast ruined castle, the castle of Count Dracula.

Commentary

From what we read in Harker's journal, it is clear that the young lawyer is a very logical, organized sort of man. Clearly, Stoker is setting up his protagonist as a very rational individual; in this way, the horror of the melodrama which will occur later will be encountered by a man who will try to combat it with common sense and logic. As a result, the terror of Stoker's narrative will become heightened and will seem more believable and less excessively hysterical. Had Stoker chosen a nervous, emotional type of man for his hero, his gothic melodrama would have become, or could have become, laughable and ludicrous. This is not the case, however; because of the carefully calculated way in which Stoker indicates and unravels the mystery of Count Dracula, he achieves a mastery over his subject matter that mitigates the raw horror and, instead, intensifies each chapter's sense of anxiety and portentous dread.

One of the first devices that Stoker uses to let us know that Harker is sensible and rational (in addition to the fact that he is a lawyer) is by having Harker recall in his journal that he spent quite a bit of time prior to his journey in the British Museum; there, he read as much as he could about the provinces through which he would be traveling (provinces originally occupied by Attila and the Huns); Harker tried his best to locate the exact locality of Castle Dracula, but unfortunately, he was not able to pinpoint the location precisely, because the castle is located in one of the "wildest and least known portions of Europe." Yet even this ominously mysterious fact does not worry Harker unduly; because he is able to use his smattering of German, he is enjoying his adventuresome trip – thus far – and his notes become more minutely descriptive and confessional as he continues; the purpose for recording as much as he can, he says, is so that he can later refresh his memory when he is telling his fiancée, Mina, about the journey.

One of the first clues in Harker's journal that suggests to us something about the terror that will soon commence concerns Harker's reaction to Transylvania itself. He notes that "every known superstition in the world is gathered into the horseshoe of the Carpathians"; he also records, again matter-of-factly, the minor annoyance of his having had "all sorts of queer dreams" recently; in addition, he heard a "dog howling all night under [his] window." He wonders, rather naively, if perhaps it was the excessive paprika in the chicken casserole which he ate for dinner that could have been responsible for his bad dreams.

CHAPTERS 2-4

Summary

Dracula's castle is described, like almost everything else, in precise detail. Harker notes the castle's great round arches, the immense iron-studded stone doors, the rattling chains, and the clanking of massive bolts, and he compares the scene with a nightmare. Dracula himself is as mysterious as his castle is. He is an old man and is clean shaven, except for a long white Victorian moustache, and he is clad all in black without "a single speck of color about him anywhere." He speaks in perfect English and welcomes Harker inside, shaking his hand with an ice-cold, vice-like grip. His house, as he guides Harker forward, is seen to be filled with long passageways and heavy doors; finally they come to a room in which a table is laid for dinner, set beside a roaring fire. The Count's greeting is so warm that Harker forgets his fears and gives Dracula the details of the real estate transfer. Dracula explains that, at present, because of gout, he will not be able to make the journey to England himself, but that one of his trusted servants will accompany Harker back to London.

After supper, Harker enjoys a cigar (Dracula does not smoke), and he studies his host: Dracula's face is strong; his high, thin nose is aquiline, and his nostrils seem to arch peculiarly; his shaggy brows almost meet, and his bushy hair seems to curl in profusion. His mouth, thick and white, covers "sharp white teeth which protrude over the lips." His ears are pale and pointed, and his cheeks are firm but extremely thin. His breath is fetid and rank. "The general effect is one of extraordinary pallor."

Both of the men hear wolves howling from far off, and Dracula is the first to speak: "The children of the night," he says, "what music they make!" Shortly, thereafter, the two men retire, and Harker records a final entry for the day: "I think strange things which I dare not confess to my own soul. God keep me, if only for the sake of those dear to me."

As Harker explores the Count's castle the next day, he notices a number of unusual, intriguing things: a meal is already prepared and is ready for him–and no servant is present. The table service is made of gold, the curtains and upholstery are made of costly fabrics, seemingly centuries old, and *nowhere* is there a mirror. To his joy, however, Harker at last discovers a vast library, and he is in the midst of perusing one of the volumes when the Count appears. Dracula tells Harker that he may go anywhere he wishes in the castle, except where the doors are locked. Then he changes the subject and reveals that he greatly fears his proposed journey to England. He feels that his mastery of the English language is insufficient. In addition, he has grown so accustomed to being a master in his own land that he dreads going to England and suddenly being a nobody. For that reason, he wants Harker to remain in the castle as long as possible in order to perfect Dracula's English pronunciation. Harker immediately agrees to do so, and thus they talk further–first, about inconsequential things, and then Dracula explains about the evil spirits in Transylvania that sometimes hold sway. There is "hardly a foot of soil" in all this region, says the Count, "that has not been enriched by the blood of men, patriots, or invaders.

Afterward, their conversation turns to England, and while it is evident that the Count is concerned that he shall, for the most part, be alone in his new surroundings, he is immensely pleased by the description of his new estate: it is surrounded by high walls, made of heavy stone, is in need of repair, but contains massive, old iron gates; it is surrounded by dense trees, and the only building in the nearby vicinity is a private lunatic asylum. "I love the shade and the shadow," Dracula says; "I am no longer young; and my heart, through years of mourning over the dead, is not attuned to mirth."

The two men talk throughout the night, and at the coming of dawn, when the cock crows, Dracula leaps up excitedly and excuses himself. Harker feels nothing tangibly amiss, but he confesses in his diary that he feels uneasy; he wishes that he were home and that he had never journeyed to Transylvania.

Next morning as Harker is shaving, his host's voice startles him, and he cuts himself. Then two unexplainable, horrible things occur. Harker realizes that, first, there is no reflection of Count Dracula in the shaving mirror; and second, when the Count sees Harker's fresh blood trickling from his chin, his eyes blaze up "with a sudden demoniac fury," and he lunges for Harker's throat. Instinctively, Harker touches his crucifix, and Dracula's fury vanishes. He counsels Harker to take care how he cuts himself in this country; then Dracula flings the shaving glass onto the courtyard stones below, where it shatters into a thousand pieces. Dracula vanishes, and Harker ponders about what has happened. He also wonders about the fact that he has never seen the Count eat or drink. Harker then explores the castle farther and finally concludes that no matter how many beautiful vistas which he is able to see from the battlements, the castle is a veritable prison, and he is its prisoner.

After Harker realizes that he is indeed a prisoner in Dracula's castle, he succumbs to panic and feelings of helplessness; momentarily, he believes that he is going mad, but he recovers almost instantly and tries to rationally analyze what he must do to escape and survive. More than anything else, Harker realizes that he will "need all [his] brains to get through." Ironically, since Harker is not a religious man, he is grateful for the crucifix which was given to him; it is "a comfort and a strength."

A good night's sleep is virtually impossible for Harker, despite the fact that he has placed the crucifix over the head of the bed; thus, he paces throughout the night, looks out of his windows, and by accident, he sees Dracula, on two separate occasions, emerge from his room on the floor below, slither out, head downward, in lizard fashion, with his cloak spread out "around him like great wings." It is shortly afterward that Harker records in his diary that he fears for his sanity; he hopes that he does not go mad. His diary is his only solace; he turns to it "for repose."

One of Harker's favorite rooms in the castle is one that he feels was probably a woman's room; romantically, he likes to imagine that in this room "ladies sat and sung and lived sweet lives whilst their gentle breasts were sad for their menfolk away in the midst of remorseless wars." It is during one moonlight night in this room that three women appear before Harker – and whether or not this is a dream, we cannot be sure. Harker's horror, however, is quite real, and that concerns us most. Two of the women are dark, and both of them have vivid, glowing red eyes; the other woman is fair. All have "brilliant white teeth," and all of them cause a burning, sexual desire within Harker. Unexplainably, Harker finds himself allowing the fair woman to bend over him until he can feel her hot breath on his neck. As two sharp teeth touch his neck, and as he closes [his] eyes "in languorous ecstasy," waiting "with beating heart," Count Dracula suddenly sweeps in and orders the women out. But before they go, Harker notices that they grab a small bag with "some living thing within it"; with horror, Harker is sure that he hears a low wail, like that "of a half-smothered child." Then he sinks into unconsciousness.

Significantly, Harker awakens in his own bed. Perhaps the women and the gruesome bag were only part of a bad dream. Thus he steels himself for others "who are – waiting to suck [his] blood." Harker waits, and while he does so, he notices gypsies who are driving wagons filled with large, square, empty boxes. Later, he hears the muffled sounds of digging, and again, he sees the Count slither down the side of the castle, lizard-fashion, wearing Harker's clothes and carrying "the terrible bag." A howling dog cries far below in the valley. The horror overcomes Harker; locked in his prison, he sits down and cries.

It is then that he hears a woman below, crying out for her child, tearing her hair, beating her breasts, and "beating her naked hands against the door." Within moments, a pack of wolves pour "like a pent-up dam" into the courtyard. Then they stream away, "licking their lips."

Harker has no choice; he must try to encounter Dracula during daylight. Therefore, he crawls out his window and descends, perilously, until he reaches the Count's room. Oddly, it is empty, and it seems "to have never been used"; everything is covered with dust, including a "great heap of gold in one corner." Seeing an open door, Harker follows a circular stairway down through dark, tunnel-like passages; with every step, he becomes more aware of a "deathly, sickly odour, the odour of old earth newly turned."

In the vaults below, Harker discovers fifty boxes, and in one of them, he finds the Count, apparently asleep, even though his eyes are "open and strong." Horrified, he flees to his room and tries to decide what he must do.

On June 29th, he reveals the full extent of his terror. He is terribly afraid; if he had a gun, he would try to kill the Count, but at this point, he believes that the Count is supernatural and that bullets would have no effect on him. Yet when the Count appears, he bids Harker goodbye, assuring him that a carriage will take him to the Borgo Pass and from there, he will be able to return to England.

Later, Harker opens his door and sees "the three terrible women licking their lips." He throws himself on the floor, imploring heaven to save him until he can escape the following day.

Not surprisingly, Harker wakes early, scales down the wall, and once more he finds the Count laid out in one of the large wooden boxes. Curiously, the old man looks "as if his youth [had] been half renewed." The reason is clear. He has been renewed by blood. On his lips are thick blotches of fresh blood which trickle from the corners of his mouth and run over his chin and neck. Dracula is gorged with blood, "like a filthy leech." The thought of Harker's assisting this monster to travel to England and satiate his lust on unsuspecting English men and women so horrifies Harker that he seizes a shovel and slashes madly at the Count's "hateful face." The Count's mad eyes so paralyze Harker, however, that the blow only grazes the Count's forehead. Hearing voices, Harker flees to the Count's room, where he hears the boxes below being filled with earth and the covers nailed shut. Then he hears the sound of wheels in the driveway, the crack of whips, and a chorus of gypsies. Now Harker is convinced that he is absolutely alone, a prisoner, and Dracula is off for England to wreak his evil. Yet Harker is still determined to at least try and escape and take some of the gold with him. He is sure that this castle is a nest for the "devil and his children," and he cannot remain in it a moment longer. The precipice which he must confront is steep and high, but he must attempt it at all costs. The last entry in his journal, at this point, is desperate: "Good-bye, all! Mina!"

Commentary

These three chapters set the tone for all subsequent treatments of the Dracula legend. That is, whereas many works based on Count Dracula will alter the story significantly, most of the subsequent treatments of this legend will have some of the incidents found in these chapters. They include (1) an emissary (sometimes the pattern includes unsuspecting travelers) who is in a foreign land to contact the mysterious Count Dracula, who has bought some property in England. The young man, therefore, has come to finalize the arrangements with Dracula. (2) The setting is always someplace in Transylvania, a land sparsely populated and filled with howling wolves. It is also often remote and strange and unfamiliar, with no main roads to enter or depart by. (3) Everything is strange, even the language, which prevents the emissary from communicating with the natives (The natives are always of peasant stock and extremely superstitious and often xenophobic). (4) The representative usually stops in some remote inn, without such modern conveniences as telephones, where a carriage with an inscrutable driver will take him to the Borgo Pass. (5) The peasants will offer him various charms to ward off *vampires*, a word that strikes fear into the peasants. (6) The Borgo Pass is well known for mysterious happenings and the emissary usually arrives about midnight, a time when evil spirits have free reign in the world. (7) The emissary is met by someone working for the Count and is taken to the Count's castle. (8) The castle is a decaying edifice, located at the top of a tall mountain amid a desolate area, where one can gain access to the castle only by a steep, narrow road. The castle is a landmark, but few people tour the place. (9) Everything is old and musty in the castle. (10) Count Dracula is seen only at nighttime, and the emissary never sees him eat anything even though there is plenty of freshly prepared food. (11) The narrator usually sees Count Dracula performing some act which would be considered supernatural, such as slithering down the sheer precipice of the castle in a "bat-like" manner. (12) Often there is the presence of a female vampire (or vampires), who will attempt to seduce the narrator. (13) Usually the emissary is imprisoned in the castle and must effect his own escape.

Other factors of a lesser nature can be included, factors such as the narrator's explorations of the castle and his discovery of many coffins or boxes of dirt or the proliferation of bats about the castle, the eerie noises, and the mysterious absence of mirrors (since vampires do not cast a reflection in a mirror), and sometimes there are the cries of young babies and the presence of blood at unexpected places. Therefore, the individual writer can utilize as many of the above archetypical patterns as he or she so chooses.

CHAPTERS 5 & 6

Summary

The scene abruptly shifts from Transylvania to London, and the story of Mina Murray (later Mina Harker) and Lucy Westenra is introduced. The story in the following few chapters is presented through a series of letters between Mina Murray and Lucy Westenra, and also through journal entries of various characters, as well as by newspaper articles and even a ship's log. In these chapters we are also introduced to Dr. John Seward whom Lucy describes as "one of the most resolute men" she ever saw, "yet the most calm"; Arthur Holmwood, whom Lucy chooses to marry; and Quincey P. Morris, a Texan, a friend of Arthur Holmwood; and Dr. Seward, director of a lunatic asylum. All of these characters will figure prominently in the story.

Mina Murray, an assistant "schoolmistress," is engaged to Jonathan Harker. In Mina's letter to her dear friend Lucy, she tells of Jonathan's recent letters from Transylvania which assure her that he is well and will soon be returning home. (These are early letters from Jonathan, of course.) Mina's first letter is dated a few days after Jonathan's arrival at Castle Dracula.

Lucy's reply reveals that she is in love with a Mr. Arthur Holmwood, a "tall, curly haired man." She also mentions a doctor whom she would like Mina to meet. The doctor, John Seward, is "handsome" and "really clever," twenty-nine years old, and the administrator of a lunatic asylum. At the conclusion of Lucy's letter, we learn that Mina and Lucy have been friends since childhood and that each depends on the other for happiness.

In Lucy's next letter to Mina, Lucy reveals to us that she will be twenty years old in three months. On this particular day (the 24th of May), she has had no less than *three* marriage proposals, and she is ecstatic. The first proposal was from Dr. Seward, whom she turned down. The second proposal came from the American, Quincey P. Morris. She finds the American to be gallant and romantic, yet she feels that she must turn him down as well. The third proposal came from Arthur Holmwood, whose proposal she accepted.

Following the exchange of letters between Mina and Lucy, we have an excerpt from Dr. Seward's diary (kept on a phonograph) from the 25th of May, the day following his proposal to Lucy. Dr. Seward reveals his depression over Lucy's rejection, but he will resign himself to his vocation. Dr. Seward also mentions, most importantly, his curiosity about one of his patients. This patient's name is R. M. Renfield, who is fifty-nine years old and a man of "great physical strength." Dr. Seward notes that Renfield is "morbidly excitable" and has "periods of gloom ending in some fixed idea" which the doctor is unable to determine. Seward concludes the entry by stating that he believes Renfield to be potentially dangerous.

Following Seward's entry is a letter from the American, Quincey P. Morris, to Arthur Holmwood, dated May 25th. In the letter, Quincey asks Arthur to drink with him to drown his sorrows over a woman's rejection – and also, he proposes to drink to Arthur's happiness. Quincey also reveals the name of another fellow who will be present, one who also happens to wish to drown his sorrows – Dr. Seward.

Mina's journal of the 24th of July comes from Whitby, a town located in northeast England, on the seacoast; her description of Whitby would pass for one in a travel guide. Of special note is Mina's description of the ruins of Whitby Abbey: Mina says that it is a "most noble ruin . . . full of beautiful and romantic bits," and she mentions the legend of a "white lady" who is seen in one of the Abbey's windows. She also mentions a large graveyard which lies above the town and has a "full view of the harbor."

Of the friends whom Mina makes at Whitby, she is most charmed by a "funny old man" named Mr. Swales. Mr. Swales is very old, for Mina tells us that his face is "all gnarled and twisted like the bark of a tree," and that Swales brags that he is almost one hundred years old. He is a skeptical person and scoffs at the legend of the "white lady" of Whitby Abbey.

A week later, Mina and Lucy are on the hillside above Whitby talking to old Mr. Swales. Lucy playfully refers to him as the "Sir Oracle" of the area. Mina mentions Lucy's robust health and her happy spirits since coming to Whitby. On this day, Mr. Swales refuses to tell Mina and Lucy about a legend which he scoffs at. The legend involves and maintains that many of the graves in the yard are actually empty. This notion is, of course, preposterous to Mr. Swales, and he tells the ladies that they should not believe the silly superstitions of the area.

Mina reports that Lucy and Arthur are preparing for their wedding and that she still hasn't heard from Jonathan for a month;

interestingly, the date of this entry is also the date of the last entry that Jonathan Harker made in the journal that he kept in Count Dracula's castle in Transylvania.

Dr. Seward, meanwhile, reports that the case of Renfield is becoming more and more curious. Seward reports that Renfield has developed qualities of selfishness, secrecy, and dubiousness; in addition, Renfield has pets of odd sorts; presently, Renfield's hobby is catching flies, and he has a large number of them. When Seward demands that Renfield get rid of them, Renfield asks for a delay of three days. Two weeks later, Seward reports that Renfield has become interested in spiders and has "several very big fellows in a box." Evidently, Renfield is feeding the flies to the spiders and also munching on the flies himself. About ten days later, Seward reports that the spiders are becoming a great nuisance and that he has ordered Renfield to get rid of them. As Seward is issuing this demand, a fly buzzes into the room and Renfield catches it and "exultantly" eats it. Renfield keeps a notebook in which whole pages are filled with masses of numbers, as if it is an account book; we can assume that he is totaling up the number of flies that he has eaten.

A week later, Seward discovers that Renfield also has a pet sparrow and that Renfield's supply of spiders has diminished; it would seem that Renfield also maintains a supply of flies for the spiders by tempting them with pieces of food. About ten days later, Seward reports that Renfield has "a whole colony of sparrows" and that the supply of flies and spiders is almost depleted.

Fawning like a dog, Renfield begs Seward for a nice little kitten which he can "feed – and feed – and feed." Seward refuses Renfield's request, and Renfield immediately becomes hostile and threatening. Seward fears that Renfield is an "undeveloped homicidal maniac." Upon returning to Renfield's cell a few hours later, Seward discovers Renfield in the corner, "gnawing his fingers." Renfield immediately begs for a kitten again. The next day, Renfield is spreading sugar on the window sill, evidently trying to catch flies again. Seward is surprised that the room is empty of birds, and when Renfield is asked where they are, he responds that they have all flown away. Seward is disconcerted, however, when he sees a few feathers and some blood on Renfield's pillow. A few hours later, an attendant tells Seward that Renfield vomited and disgorged a large quantity of feathers. That evening, Seward orders that Renfield be given a strong opiate to make him sleep. Seward decides to classify Renfield as a "zoöphagous [life eating] maniac." Seward defines this phenomenon as a person who tries "to absorb as many lives as he can," one who has laid himself out to achieve it in a cumulative way. Seward is thrilled with the possibility that he might advance this branch of science and, thus, become famous.

The novel now shifts back to Mina Murray's journal, July 26th, about a week after Seward's last entry. Mina voices concern about not hearing from Jonathan Harker and also, curiously, about Lucy. Additionally, Mina is confused as to why she hasn't heard from Jonathan because yesterday, Jonathan's employer, Mr. Hawkins, sent her a letter from Jonathan, a letter that was written at Count Dracula's castle. The letter consists of only one line, a statement that he is starting home. Mina notes that this extreme brevity is totally unlike Jonathan.

Mina is also concerned about Lucy because Lucy has once again "taken to her old habit of walking in her sleep." In a late entry of the 6th of August, Mina notes that the fishermen claim that a harsh storm is approaching. Old Mr. Swales tells her that he has never felt closer to death and that he is tired of fighting it. He also senses approaching calamity and doom: "There is something in that wind . . . that sounds, and looks, and tastes, and smells like death." At the end of the entry, she reports sighting a strange ship which old Mr. Swales says is a Russian ship.

Commentary

Stoker continues with his epistolary style, continuing in the tradition of having two young, naive ladies corresponding about love and life. These innocent girls will very soon become involved in the horror which Dracula brings. Stoker contrasts their innocence with the approaching plague of horror and evil, a typically gothic pattern of narrative; it would not be dramatically effective to have depraved characters confront the evil menace.

The setting is a typical one for the gothic novel. We leave the hustle and bustle of a metropolitan city and journey to an isolated city, replete with legends of empty graves, sepulchral old natives, and legends of dead people who haunt huge old houses. Furthermore, any type of ghost story should be set in some place far from civilization, and here at Whitby, where there are rambling old houses, sleepwalking, and graveyards, we have a perfect gothic setting.

The story of Renfield foreshadows the social disruption and insanity which will accompany Dracula's descent upon England. This is further symbolized by Renfield's desire for blood and the sucking of fresh blood, which will be Dracula's, or the vampire's, goal. Renfield can be seen as an archetype of "the predecessor" (such as John the Baptist) because Renfield prepares us for the imminent arrival of his "lord" and "master," Dracula. Stoker will continue to pervert Christian myths throughout the novel. Dracula is a satanic figure, and the horrors of Renfield are maudlin, compared to the greater horror which is Dracula himself.

Lucy's sleepwalking also prefigures the arrival of Count Dracula. As it happens, the day that she begins sleepwalking will closely correspond to the day that Dracula's ship crosses the straits of Gibraltar into Western civilization. And it will be because of her sleepwalking that she will become a member of the "Un-Dead."

Old Mr. Swales is the archetypal prophetic figure, one who senses and can articulate the approaching doom and horror, yet one whose exhortations and prophesies are ignored or remain misunderstood by the populace.

CHAPTERS 7 & 8

Summary

Utilizing the narrative device of a newspaper clipping (dated August 8th), the story of the landing of Count Dracula's ship is presented. The report indicates that the recent storm, one of the worst storms on record, was responsible for the shipwreck of a strange Russian vessel. The article also mentions several observations which indicate the vessel's strange method of navigation; we learn that observers feel that the captain had to be mad because in the midst of the storm the ship's sails were wholly unfurled.

Many people who witnessed the approach of the strange vessel were gathered on one of Whitby's piers to await the ship's arrival. By the light of a spotlight, witnesses noticed that "lashed to the helm was a corpse, with drooping head, which swung horribly to and fro" as the ship rocked. As the vessel violently ran aground, "an immense dog sprang up on deck from below," jumped from the ship, and ran off. Upon closer inspection, it was discovered that the man lashed to the wheel (the helm) had a crucifix clutched in his hand. According to a local doctor, the man had been dead for at least two days. Coast Guard officials discovered a bottle in the dead man's pocket, carefully sealed, which contained a roll of paper.

In a newspaper article the next day, it is revealed that the ship, a schooner, was a Russian vessel, one from Varna, called the *Demeter*. The only cargo on board was a "ballast of silver sand" and "a number of great wooden boxes filled with mould." It is revealed that the cargo was consigned to a Whitby solicitor, Mr. S. F. Billington, who has claimed the boxes. The bizarre circumstances of the ship's arrival have been the talk about town for the last few days, and there has also been some interest as to the whereabouts of the big dog which jumped ashore on the first night. The dog has disappeared, and some citizens are worried that the dog may be dangerous. Reportedly, a half-breed mastiff was found dead, its throat torn out and its belly split open.

The narrative continues with excerpts from the *Demeter*'s log. The log begins on the 6th of July, which would be a week after Jonathan Harker's last entry in his journal. According to the log entries, all is calm aboard the ship for several days. On the 16th of July, however, one crew member is found missing, and the log indicates that all the sailors are downcast and anxious. The next day, the 17th of July, a sailor reports seeing a "tall, thin man, who was not like any of the crew, come up the companionway, and go along the deck forward and disappear." Yet no one, upon inspection of the ship, is to be found.

Five days later, on the 22nd of July, the ship passes Gibraltar and sails out through the Straits with apparently no further problems. Two days later, however, another man is reported lost, and the remaining men grow panicky and frightened. Five days later, another sailor is missing. On the 30th of July, only the captain, his mate, and two crew members are left. On the 2nd of August, another crew member disappears. At midnight on the next night, the remaining deck hand disappears, and the captain and the mate are the only remaining men aboard. The captain reports that the mate is haggard and close to madness. In a panic, the mate, a Roumanian, hisses, "*It* is here." The mate thinks that "it" is in the hold, perhaps "in one of the boxes." The mate descends into the hold, only to come flying from the hold moments later, screaming in terror, telling the captain, "He is there.

I know the secret now." In despair, the mate throws himself overboard, preferring drowning to a confrontation with "the thing." Since the captain feels that it is his duty to remain with the ship, he vows to tie his hands to the wheel and take the ship to port. At this point, the log ends.

The log of the *Demeter* stirs up a great deal of controversy, and most of the townsfolk regard the captain as a hero. The reporter ends his narration by stating that the great dog has not yet been found.

The narrative shifts then to Mina's journal (August 8th), the day of the great storm. Lucy is still sleepwalking, and Mina has yet to hear from Jonathan.

On the 10th of August, Mina indicates that the burial of the sea captain was on this day and that Lucy is very upset about the events of the last few days. In a shocking revelation, we learn that old Mr. Swales was found dead this morning, near the graveyard, at the seat where Lucy and Mina would often visit with him. According to the doctor, the old man must have "fallen back in the seat in some sort of fright" because his neck was broken.

Mina's journal for the 10th of August concludes with the observation that Lucy is happy and seems better in body and in spirit than she has for quite some time. The next entry is a few hours later; at 3 A.M., Mina awakened with a horrible sense of fear and discovered that Lucy's bed was empty. After satisfying herself that Lucy was nowhere to be found inside the house, she threw a heavy shawl about herself and headed outdoors to search for Lucy. While searching, it occurred to Mina that Lucy might have gone to their favorite place, the seat on the hill where old Mr. Swales was found. She looked towards the hill where the seat was located and, under the light of a "beautiful moon," she saw on the seat a half-reclining figure, "snowy white." Above the figure, "something dark" was bending over the reclining figure. Mina raced to the spot. When she approached the seat, Mina saw something "long and black" bent over the half reclining figure. Mina called to Lucy in fright, and "the thing raised a head." Mina could see "a white face and red, gleaming eyes." By the time Mina reached the seat, the moonlight was so brilliant that Mina could see that Lucy was alone. It appeared that Lucy was merely asleep, but her breathing was hesitant and coming in long, heavy gasps; then Lucy shuddered and covered her throat with her hand. Mina threw her shawl over Lucy to warm her, and Lucy pulled the shawl up about her neck as though she were cold. Mina accounts for the two puncture wounds in Lucy's throat as the result of pin pricks caused when Mina was trying to pin a shawl around Lucy's exposed neck. Mina then escorts Lucy back home and puts her back to bed. Just before falling asleep, Lucy begs Mina not to tell anyone of the incident.

That morning (August 11th) Lucy looks better to Mina than she has for weeks. Mina berates herself for wounding Lucy with the safety pin, for again she notices the two little red pin pricks on Lucy's neck, "and on the band of her nightdress was a drop of blood." Lucy casually laughs off Mina's concern. The rest of the day is spent happily, and Mina expects a restful night.

In her journal entry of the next day, however, Mina indicates that her expectations were wrong. Twice that night Mina discovered that Lucy was awake and trying to leave the room. Yet, the next morning, Lucy was, seemingly, the picture of health to Mina.

The 13th of August is a quiet day, yet that night Mina discovers Lucy sitting up in bed in a dazed sleep, "pointing to the window." Mina goes to the window, and in the brilliant moonlight she notices "a great bat" flitting about in circles. Evidently the bat is frightened by the sudden appearance of Mina at the window and flies off.

The next day at sunset, Mina indicates that she and Lucy spent the day at a favorite spot on the East Cliff, and, at sunset, Lucy made a most unusual remark: "His red eyes again! They are just the same." At the moment when Lucy utters this phrase, Mina notices that Lucy's eyes are directed towards their favorite seat, "whereon was a dark figure seated alone." To Mina, the stranger's eyes appeared for a moment "like burning flames." Later, the two return home and say no more about the incident.

After seeing Lucy to bed that night, Mina decided to go for a short stroll. Coming home in the bright moonlight, she glanced up at their bedroom window and noticed Lucy's head leaning out. Mina thought that Lucy was looking for her, but she was not – Lucy did not even notice Mina. She appeared, in fact, to be fast asleep. Curiously, seated on the window sill next to her was something that looked like a "good sized bird." Running upstairs to the bedroom in a panic, Mina discovered that Lucy was now back in her bed – asleep, but holding her hand to her throat as if chilled. Mina chooses not to awaken her, yet she notices, much to her dismay, that Lucy looks pale and haggard. Mina attributes this to Lucy's fretting about something.

On the next day (15th of August), Mina notices that Lucy is "languid and tired" and that she slept later than normal. Mina receives a bit of unexpected and shocking news from Mrs. Westenra, Lucy's mother. Mrs. Westenra's doctor has informed her that she has only a few months to live because of a heart condition.

Two days later, Mina is despondent. She has had no news from Jonathan yet, and Lucy seems to be growing weaker and weaker by the day. Mina cannot understand Lucy's decline, for she eats well and sleeps well and gets plenty of exercise. Yet at night, Mina has heard her awaken as if gasping for air, and just last night, she found Lucy leaning out of the open window again; Lucy was incredibly weak and her breath came with much difficulty. Inspecting Lucy's throat as she lay asleep, Mina noticed that the puncture wounds had not healed; if anything, they were larger than before and the edges were pale and faintly puckered. "They were like little white dots with red centers."

In a letter dated the 17th of August, Mr. S. F. Billington (to whom the boxes from the *Demeter* were consigned) orders the boxes to be delivered to Carfax, near Purfleet, in London.

Mina's journal (August 18th) records that Lucy is looking better and slept well the last night. Lucy seems to have come to terms with the night when she was found sleepwalking. Lucy spends most of her time thinking of her fiancé, Arthur. Lucy feels that the recent events are like a dream, yet she has a "vague memory of something long and dark with red eyes . . . and something very sweet and very bitter all around . . . sinking into deep green water." Her "soul seemed to go out from [her] body and float about in the air." She tells Mina there was suddenly "a sort of agonizing feeling." And then Mina woke her.

On the 19th of August, Mina receives news of Jonathan – he is in a hospital in Budapest. Mina intends to leave the next morning to go to Budapest to be with him; Jonathan apparently has been hospitalized because of brain fever. In a letter from a Sister Agatha, Mina is warned that she should be prepared to spend some time at the hospital, for Jonathan's illness is very serious.

The narrative shifts then to Dr. Seward's diary. Renfield, it seems, has had a swift and drastic change in personality. He has periods of excitement, and he acts as if he were a caged animal. He had been respectful, but recently, he has become quite "haughty." He has told Seward that "the Master is at hand." Dr. Seward attributes Renfield's condition to a "religious mania." Renfield's pets (the spiders, flies, and sparrows) are no longer important to him. Later that night, Renfield escapes. Dr. Seward and several attendants follow Renfield to Carfax (the destination of the fifty boxes of earth belonging to Count Dracula). Following him onto the grounds, Seward finds Renfield "pressed close against the old iron-bound oak door of the chapel," apparently talking to someone. Renfield is apparently addressing someone whom he calls "Master"; Renfield seems to consider himself a slave. Dr. Seward and the attendants put a restraint on Renfield and return him to his cell. There, Renfield says that he "shall be patient, Master."

Commentary

Once again Stoker relies on clever stylistic devices to add verisimilitude to his story. By using newspaper clippings, the ship's log, the medical journal, excerpts from telegrams and diaries, he builds a cumulative picture of events as though they might really have happened and, thus, he gives greater credence to this improbable story.

The ship that was sighted at the end of Chapter 6 has turned out to be the ship which was carrying the loads of dirt from Count Dracula's estate, the cargo that Jonathan Harker saw being loaded on wagons in Transylvania. Apparently, Count Dracula himself is "residing" in one of these boxes. The storm, the howling dogs, and the mysterious disappearance of the sailors—all are symbolic of the approaching evil which is represented by Count Dracula. It is clear that Dracula is a harbinger of the natural catastrophes which are occurring. His evil presence is felt by old Mr. Swales, who at his advanced age cannot withstand the horrors represented by the arrival of Dracula and is found dead, murdered to make it seem as though he were killed accidentally. It can be assumed that the mysterious dog that came from the ship was Dracula himself in one of his guises, and that it was responsible for knocking the old man down and causing his death. Many supernatural things, like Mr. Swales' death, are never fully explained by Stoker, leaving all the events surrounded by an aura of superstition and mystery.

The calm Victorian life, filled with all of the amenities of life, is being penetrated by everything which Dracula represents, and the disruption is seen mainly in the manner in which he "penetrates" a young virgin's (Lucy's) neck, sucking both life and blood from her.

The illness of Arthur Holmwood's father (only slightly mentioned), as well as the approaching death of Lucy's mother, seem cabalistically linked to the approach and arrival of Count Dracula, and, thus, by the end of the novel we will see that both Lucy and her mother have become victims of the intruding spectre of horror. Dracula is more than just a vampire, more than just a satanic presence affecting only a few; he is also a symbol of total social disruption and chaos. If not stopped, he will destroy all of Victorian society. Count Dracula's appearance and his satanic presence – his black clothes, his fiery red eyes, and his pale features – are a total contrast to the winsome, innocent, and virginal presence of the two ladies (Lucy and Mina) who represent purity.

Once again, Stoker inverts the traditional Christian myth when Renfield anticipates and looks forward to the arrival of his "lord and master" in the person of Count Dracula. Stoker, in an interesting choice of phraseology, considers Renfield's behavior at Carfax as though Renfield is experiencing a "Real Presence," as though Dracula were the (perverted) Holy Ghost. The entire scene is a perversion of the Catholic communion, wherein the Real Presence of the Holy Ghost is present each time that the Eucharist is administered.

In terms of the narrative structure so far, we don't know *why* Count Dracula left Transylvania to come to England – rather than go somewhere else, or even why he had to leave his native country. However, in these chapters, we find out that Jonathan Harker *did* escape, but his method of escape will never be revealed to us; remember that when we last saw him, he was a prisoner in Dracula's castle, surrounded by wolves and supernatural beings. Yet suddenly, without explanation, he appears in Budapest, where he is cared for by nurses.

CHAPTERS 9 & 10

Summary

In a letter from Budapest, Mina tells Lucy that she has arrived safely and that she has found Jonathan Harker greatly changed. He is only a shadow of his former self, and he remembers very little of what has happened to him; he suffered a terrible shock, and his brain has a mental block against whatever caused his present condition.

Sister Agatha, who has attended him, has told Mina that he raved and ranted about dreadful and unspeakable things, so dreadful that she often had "to cross herself." Sister Agatha maintains that "his fear is of great and horrible things, which no mortal can think of." Mina notices a notebook and wonders if she could look through it for some clue as to what happened; Jonathan tells her that he has had brain fever, and he thinks that the cause of the brain fever *might* be recorded in the notebook. However, he does *not* ever want to read the contents of the book *himself*. Thus he gives the journal to Mina and says that if she wants to read it she may, but he never wants to read it lest it cause some horror in their married life.

Mina informs Lucy that she and Jonathan have decided to get married immediately, and, that very afternoon, the marriage ceremony was performed. As a wedding gift, Mina took the notebook, wrapped it, tied it, and sealed it in wax, using her wedding ring as the seal, saying that she would *never* open it unless it were for his—Jonathan's—sake. After reading her friend's letter, Lucy sends Mina a letter of congratulations, telling her that she herself is feeling quite healthy.

Dr. Seward records in his diary that Renfield has now grown very quiet and often murmurs to himself, "Now I can wait, now I can wait." He does not speak to anyone, even when he is offered a kitten or a full grown cat as a pet. He responds, "I don't take any stock in cats. I have more to think of now."

This has happened for three nights; now, Seward plans to arrange a way for Renfield to escape so that they can follow him. At an unexpected moment, however, Renfield escapes. The attendant follows him to Carfax, where he is again pressed against the old chapel door.

When Renfield sees Dr. Seward, he tries to attack him, but is restrained. Renfield grows strangely calm, and Dr. Seward becomes aware that Renfield is staring at something in the moonlit sky. Upon following his gaze, Seward can see nothing, however, but an exceptionally large bat.

Lucy Westenra, (on the 24th of August) records in her diary that she has been dreaming, as she did earlier at Whitby (she is now at Hillingham, another of the houses which her family owns). Also, she notes that her mother's health is declining. On the night of the 25th, she writes that she awoke around midnight to the sound of something scratching and flapping at the window. When she awoke in the morning, she was pale, and her throat pained her severely.

Arthur Holmwood writes to Dr. Seward on the 31st of August, asking him to visit Lucy and examine her. Then, the next day, he telegrams Dr. Seward to inform him that he has been called to his father's bedside, where he wants Dr. Seward to contact him.

On the 2nd of September, Dr. Seward writes to Arthur Holmwood that Lucy's health does not conform to any malady that he knows of, and that Lucy is somewhat reluctant to have him examine her completely. Dr. Seward is concerned about her "somewhat bloodless condition" because there are no signs of anemia. Lucy complains of difficulty in breathing, lethargic sleep, and dreams that frighten her. Dr. Seward is so concerned that he has sent for his old friend and master, the famous Professor Van Helsing of Amsterdam. The doctor is a profound philosopher, a metaphysician, and one of the most advanced scientists of his day.

In a letter of response, Dr. Van Helsing tells Dr. Seward that his affairs will allow him to come immediately, and that he is happy to do Dr. Seward a favor since Dr. Seward once saved his life. Consequently, Dr. Seward is able to write to Arthur Holmwood on the 3rd of September that Dr. Van Helsing has already seen Lucy and that he too is concerned about her condition, yet he has not said what is wrong with Lucy, except that there is no apparent functional cause of her illness. However, Dr. Van Helsing insists that a telegram be sent to him every day in Amsterdam letting him know about Lucy's condition.

In his diary, Dr. Seward notes that Renfield is often becoming violent at the stroke of noon and that he often howls like a wolf, disturbing the other patients. Later, the same day, he seems very contented, "catching flies and eating them." He has more sugar now and is reaping quite a harvest of flies, keeping them in a box as he did earlier. He asks for more sugar, which Dr. Seward promises to get for him. At midnight, Dr. Seward records another change in the patient. Visiting Renfield at sunset, he witnesses Renfield trying "to grab the sun" just as it sinks; then Renfield sinks to the floor. Rising, Renfield dusts the sugar and crumbs from his ledge, tosses all his flies out the window, and says, "I'm sick of all that rubbish." Dr. Seward wonders if the sun (or the moon) has any influence on Renfield's "paroxysms of sudden passion."

Dr. Seward sends telegrams on the 4th, 5th, and 6th of September to Dr. Van Helsing, the final one being a desperate plea for Dr.

Van Helsing to visit Lucy, for her condition has become much worse. Seward then sends a letter to Arthur, telling him that Lucy's condition is worse and that Van Helsing is coming to attend her. Seward cannot tell Lucy's mother about the problem because of the old woman's heart condition.

In his diary, Dr. Seward says that when Van Helsing arrived he was admonished to keep everything about this case a secret until they are certain about what is going on. Dr. Seward is anxious to know as much as possible about the case, but Van Helsing thinks that it is too premature to discuss it. When they reach Lucy's room, Dr. Seward is horrified by Lucy's ghastly pale, white face, the prominence of her bones, and her painful breathing. Observing Lucy's condition, Van Helsing frantically realizes that she must be given an immediate blood transfusion or she will die. Dr. Seward is prepared to give blood himself when Arthur suddenly arrives, volunteering that he will give "the last drop of blood in my body for her."

While Dr. Van Helsing is administering the transfer of blood from Arthur to Lucy, he gives Lucy a narcotic to allow her to sleep. After awhile, the transfusion restores color to Lucy's face, while Arthur, meanwhile, grows paler and paler. During the transfusion, the scarf around Lucy's throat falls away, and Dr. Seward notices the red marks on Lucy's throat. Later, Van Helsing asks Seward what he thinks about the marks. As they examine the wounds, they notice that they occur "just over the external jugular vein . . . two punctures, not large, but not wholesome looking." There is no sign of disease, and Seward wonders if this is not how the blood is lost. Van Helsing has to leave, and so he orders Seward to stay all night and watch over Lucy. The next morning (September 8th), Seward thinks Lucy looks better. He recalls the conversation of the evening before, when Lucy told him she did not like to go to sleep because "all that weakness comes to me in sleep." However, when Seward promised to stay with her all night, she slept soundly.

Next day, Dr. Seward had to work all day at the asylum, and that night, the 9th of September, he was extremely exhausted by work and the lack of sleep. Therefore, when Lucy showed him a room next to hers, a room with a sofa, he instinctively stretched out and fell asleep. That night, Lucy recorded in her diary how safe she feels with Dr. Seward sleeping close by.

Dr. Seward records in his diary that early on the morning of September 10th, he was awakened by the gentle hand of Dr. Van Helsing, and together they went to visit Lucy. They found her – horribly white, with shrunken gums, lips pale and blue, and looking as though she were a corpse. Immediately, they realized that another transfusion would be essential. This time, Dr. Seward is the only person available for giving blood, and he does so, "for the woman he loved." Van Helsing reminds Seward that nothing is to be said of this. Again they examine the little punctures in her throat; the wounds now have a "ragged, exhausted appearance at their edges."

In the afternoon, Van Helsing is with Lucy when the professor opens a large bundle. He opens it, hands Lucy the contents, and instructs Lucy to wear the flowers around her neck; Lucy, recognizing that "the flowers" are common garlic, thinks that he is joking. Van Helsing tells her that he is *not* joking; he says that the garlic is a special garlic, coming all the way from Haarlem (a town in Holland). Dr. Seward skeptically observes all of this, wondering if Van Helsing is "working some spell to keep out an evil spirit." Van Helsing places other bits of garlic around the room, and when they leave he tells Dr. Seward that he will be able to sleep peacefully tonight since all is well.

Commentary

Jonathan Harker's journal ended on the 30th of June, and it is still with him in the hospital, sealed and to be opened and transcribed later by Mina. The entire novel, then, is, to a large degree, held together by Harker's journal, and his observations become instrumental in resolving the mystery of Dracula. Throughout these two chapters, Lucy's health declines and improves, only to decline again. Constant emphasis is given to the two small wounds on her neck, and the reader must assume, although the author does not state it, that the expansion of the wounds and the decline of Lucy's health is a result of the vampire's repeated bloodsucking.

In addition to focusing on bloodsucking, these chapters include other examples of the Vampire-Gothic tradition. There is Renfield, who howls at noon (Dracula's powers are weakest then), yet Renfield is calm at sunset. There is also the presence of bats, as well as other mysterious "noises." Mainly, however, these chapters are concerned with the transfusion of blood into Lucy. Of course, Stoker is playing on the notion of a *lover's life's blood*. Recall that Arthur declares, "My life is hers, and I would give the last drop of blood in my body for her." The same thing, in a perverted sense, can be said for Lucy's blood, which is given to her "demon lover," the vampire. The same thing is happening when Dr. Seward gives *his* blood to his beloved Lucy, and finally, in future chapters, Van Helsing, who has learned to love Lucy as a daughter, will gladly give *his* blood to save her. Each time, Van Helsing points out that the blood is from a strong, powerful, virile young man, yet he is continually vexed as to how the lady's strength disappears. Of note here is the fact that it was dangerous to give such transfusions, because if the blood wasn't of a matching type, it could have possibly killed her. In emergencies, however, any blood is usually given to a patient if a transfusion will, hopefully, save a life.

CHAPTERS 11-13

Summary

On the 12th of September, Lucy is perplexed by the presence of the garlic flowers, but she has such trust in Van Helsing that she is not frightened to fall asleep that night.

In Dr. Seward's diary, we learn that he picked up Van Helsing and went to see Lucy the next day. They met Mrs. Westenra in the hall and discovered that she had checked on Lucy, found the room very "stuffy," and, thus, she removed those "horrible, strong smelling flowers" from around Lucy's neck and from here and there in the room, and then opened the windows in order for the room to air out. Van Helsing was very restrained in the presence of Mrs. Westenra, but as soon as she had left, Dr. Seward saw Van Helsing break down and begin to "sob with loud, dry sobs, that seemed to come from the very wracking of his heart." He feels that they are "sore beset" by some pagan fate. He recovers, and then he rushes to Lucy's room. Lucy is on the verge of death, and Seward knows that she must have another transfusion immediately, or she will die. This time, Van Helsing must be the donor since Seward has given blood to her so recently. Later, Van Helsing gently warns Mrs. Westenra that she must *never* remove anything from Lucy's room because the "flowers" and other objects have medicinal value.

Four days later, Lucy records that she is feeling much better. Even the bats flapping at her window, the harsh voices, and the distant sounds do not bother her any more.

At this point, the story is interrupted with a newspaper article about an "escaped wolf." The article tells about a curious incident a few nights earlier. It seems that when the moon was shining one night, all of the wolves of the zoo began to howl and a "big grey dog was seen coming close to the cages where the wolves were." When the zoo keeper checked the cells at midnight, he found one of the wolves missing. Suddenly the big wolf, Bersicker, returned home, docile and peaceful, except that his head was peppered with broken glass.

Dr. Seward's diary records how, on the 17th of September, he was attacked by Renfield in his office. Renfield grabbed a knife, cut Seward's wrist rather severely, and a puddle of blood formed on the floor; Renfield then began "licking it up like a dog," murmuring over and over to himself, "The blood is life."

Van Helsing telegraphs Seward, telling him to meet him at Lucy's house that night. The telegram, however, doesn't arrive until almost morning, and Seward leaves immediately for Lucy's – on the 18th of September. On the 17th of September, at nighttime, Lucy records everything she can remember in a memorandum: she was awakened by a flapping at the window and was frightened because no one was in the house; she tried to stay awake and heard something like the howl of a dog, but it was more fierce and frightening. She looked out the window, but could see only a big bat flapping its wings. Disturbed by the noise, her mother came into the room and got into bed with her. The flapping continued, and Lucy tried to calm her mother. Suddenly there was a low howl, broken glass was flying into the room, and in the window was seen "the head of a great, gaunt, grey wolf." Lucy's mother, frightened, clutched at the wreath of garlic and tore it from Lucy's neck in fright. When the wolf drew its head back, there seemed to be a "whole myriad of little specks . . . wheeling and circling around like a pillar of dust." Lucy found her mother lying lifeless, and then Lucy lost consciousness. Upon regaining consciousness a short time later, the four household maids came in and were so frightened at the sight of Mrs. Westenra's body that Lucy instructed them to go into the dining room to fetch a glass of wine. Later, when Lucy checked on them, she found them all unconscious, and upon examining the decanter, she discovered that it reeked of laudanum (an opium and alcohol mixture used as a painkiller). Lucy realizes that she is alone in the house, and she wonders where she can hide her memorandum so that someone can find it next day.

In his diary (September 18th), Dr. Seward records that he arrives at Lucy's house but isn't admitted inside. A moment later, Van Helsing arrives, and he learns that Seward did not get the telegram instructing him to stay the night. They go to the rear of the house, break in and discover the four servant women's bodies. Running to Lucy's room, they see a horror indescribable to them. Lucy's mother is dead, partly covered with a white sheet. Lucy herself is unconscious, her throat bare, the two white wounds horribly mangled, and Lucy lifeless as a corpse. Before a transfusion can be considered, however, they must warm Lucy. They revive the maids and order them to heat water, towels, and sheets. As they are wondering how to proceed next, since neither of them can give blood at the moment, and the maids are too superstitious to be relied upon, Quincey Morris arrives. He reminds them that *he also* loved Lucy, and he will give his blood to save her. While the transfusion is taking place, Van Helsing hands Seward a piece of paper that dropped from Lucy's nightgown as they carried her to the bath. Seward reads it and is vexed by its contents. He asks Van Helsing about it. The grim reality confronting them immediately, however, is to get a certificate of death filled out for Mrs. Westenra.

Later, Quincey questions Dr. Seward about Lucy's illness; he wonders where all of the blood which she received from Arthur, Seward, and Van Helsing has gone. He is reminded of a time "on the Pampas . . . [when] one of those big bats that they call vampires" attacked one of his prize mares, and the mare had to be shot.

When Lucy awakens late in the afternoon, she feels her breast for the note (which Dr. Van Helsing returned); she finds it and tears it to pieces. That night, Lucy sleeps peacefully, but her mouth "show[s] pale gums drawn back from the teeth," which look sharper and longer than usual.

That night (September 19th) Arthur Holmwood arrives to stay with Lucy. Dr. Seward's entry for September 20th notes that he is despondent and depressed. Arthur's father's death, along with the death of Mrs. Westenra, has disheartened him, and, it seems, Lucy's condition is worsening. Arthur, Dr. Seward, and Van Helsing take turns looking over her. Van Helsing has placed garlic all around the room, as well as around Lucy's neck, and he has covered the wounds on her neck with a silk handkerchief. Lucy's canine teeth appear longer and sharper than the rest. Around midnight, Seward hears a noise outside Lucy's window, and he sees a great bat flying around. When he checks on Lucy, he discovers that she has removed the garlic from around her neck. Seward also notices that she seems to be fluctuating between two states – when she is conscious, she clutches the flowers close to her neck, but when she is unconscious, she pushes the garlic from her, as though it were abhorrent. At 6 o'clock on the morning of the 20th, when Van Helsing examines Lucy, he is shocked and calls for light. The wounds on Lucy's throat have disappeared. He announces that she will soon be dead. Arthur is awakened so that he can be with her at the end, and when he comes to her, she revives. As Arthur stoops to kiss her, Van Helsing notes that Lucy's teeth seem as though they are about to fasten onto Arthur's throat. He stops Arthur and tells him to simply hold Lucy's hand, for it will comfort her more. Seward again notices that Lucy's teeth look longer and sharper than before, and suddenly Lucy opens her eyes and says to Arthur "in a soft voluptuous voice" that Seward has never heard before, "Arthur, Oh my love, I am so glad you have come! Kiss me." As Arthur bends to kiss her, Van Helsing, in a fury of strength, flings Arthur across the room, saying, "Not for your living soul, and hers!" He then instructs Arthur to come and kiss her on the forehead, only once. Suddenly, Lucy is dead! And in death, Lucy seems to regain some of the beauty that she had in life. Seward remarks, "It is the end!" but Van Helsing replies, "Not so. It is only the beginning. We can do nothing as yet. Wait and see."

Chapter 13 begins with a continuation of Dr. Seward's diary, where we read that arrangements are made for Lucy and her mother to be buried at the same time. Meanwhile, Arthur must return to bury his father. Van Helsing, who is also a lawyer, looks through Lucy's papers and retrieves all those documents which he feels might give him a clue about her death.

That night, Seward is confused by Van Helsing's actions. Van Helsing once again takes a handful of wild garlic and places the garlic all around the room and around Lucy's coffin, and then he takes a small gold crucifix and places it over Lucy's mouth. Then he makes an astonishing request to Seward. Tomorrow, he wants Seward to help him cut off Lucy's head, take out her heart, and, as we later learn, stuff her mouth with garlic. They will have to do it after the coffin has been sealed so that Arthur and others will not see the mutilated body. Seward is confused about the need for mutilating the poor girl's body, but Van Helsing tells him to be patient about an explanation; then he reminds him of that moment when Lucy was dying, when she reached up to kiss Arthur. At that moment Lucy gained consciousness enough to thank the good doctor for his actions. He reminds Seward that "there are strange and terrible days before us."

After a good sleep, Van Helsing awakens Seward with perplexing news – someone has stolen the crucifix from Lucy's mouth during the night. Now they must wait to see what happens.

When Arthur returns, he tries to explain his total despair to Seward – he has lost his fiancée, his father, and, now, his fiancée's mother, all in the matter of just a few days. He looks at Lucy's corpse and doubts that she is really dead. That night, Van Helsing asks Arthur if he can have Lucy's personal papers, assuring him that he will examine them only to determine the cause of Lucy's death. Arthur agrees with Van Helsing's request.

Mina Harker records in her journal (September 22nd) that she and Jonathan are on the train to Exeter. They arrive soon in London and then take a bus to Hyde Park. While strolling about, Mina is alarmed when Jonathan suddenly has another "nervous fit." She follows Jonathan's gaze to discover Jonathan is staring in terror at a "tall, thin man, with a beaky nose and black moustache and pointed beard." Jonathan exclaims "It is the man himself!" In a few minutes, the man hails a carriage and leaves. Jonathan is convinced that it is Count Dracula. That night, Mina receives a telegram from Van Helsing, who informs her that Mrs. Westenra and Lucy have died.

The chapter concludes with an excerpt from the Westminster Gazette (September 25th), three days after the funeral. According to the article, the area surrounding Hampstead Hill, the area where Lucy was buried, has been terrorized by a mysterious woman whom the local children refer to as "the Bloofer Lady."

Commentary

These chapters include some of the more traditional treatments for handling or warding off the presence of vampires. Van Helsing, who is the only one knowledgeable about demonology and in particular about vampire lore, sends for garlic and hangs Lucy's entire room, especially the windows, with it; then he makes a wreath of garlic to drape around Lucy's neck, and he also places a crucifix around her neck. The garlic and the crucifix are two traditional agents that have become associated with the devices that can be used to ward off vampires.

In these chapters, it is clear that evil spirits can accomplish their aims in devious sorts of ways, as attested to by sixteenth-century legends concerning Faust. For example, even though Lucy is locked in her room and protected from the vampire by the profusion of garlic, the evil spirit of the Un-Dead is able to summon a wolf from his cage in a zoo, have him smash in a window, and thereby enable the vampire to enter the room. The smashing of the window and the wolf's horrible and terrifying attempt to enter the room cause Lucy's mother to panic and to rip the garlic away from Lucy's throat, leaving Lucy vulnerable to attack. The evil presence of the vampire manages to "materialize" inside Lucy's room, where it drugs the four household maids, thus preventing their aiding Lucy.

It is interesting to note that at this point, while we have been using the term "vampire" off-handedly, Quincey Morris's discussion of the vampire bat is the first time that the term "vampire" has actually been used in the novel. Stoker is careful to point out, or to detail, the lengthening of Lucy's canine teeth so that they resemble the archetypical vampire teeth, the teeth that the vampire uses to suck blood from its victim.

As a sidenote, it is interesting to consider that within a week we have witnessed the deaths of four people intimately associated with either Lucy or Mina: Lucy's mother, Mr. Hawkins (Jonathan's employer), and Arthur's father (Lord Godalming) have died (thus causing Arthur Holmwood to inherit the title), and, of course, Lucy herself has died.

Early in Chapter 11, when Van Helsing finds out that Lucy's mother took the garlic out of Lucy's room, Van Helsing, for the first time in his life, breaks down, loses his composure, and sobs bitterly. This is a dramatic device, used to indicate the magnitude of the evil which he is facing.

In this novel and other similar stories, Van Helsing represents those powers for good combating the powers of evil which are so dimly known and which so few people believe; thus, the deaths and Van Helsing's dejected state illustrate how completely the evil of Dracula has affected society.

As we will discover, Lucy is, in fact, the Bloofer Lady. Recall that she died on September 20th, and the first appearance of the Bloofer Lady occurred after Lucy's burial on the 22nd; thus, Lucy has risen from the dead after three days – in a dreadful perversion of the Christian Resurrection.

CHAPTERS 14-16

Summary

Mina decides to transcribe the journal which Jonathan kept at the Castle Dracula in Transylvania. On the 24th of September, she receives a letter from Dr. Van Helsing asking her if he may discuss Lucy's illness with her. Mina agrees to see him and, that day, Van Helsing arrives. This is the first time that Mina has met Van Helsing, and she gives him Jonathan's journal, which she has finished transcribing. Later that day, Mina receives a note from Van Helsing in which he expresses an intense desire to meet Jonathan. Mina suggests that Van Helsing come for breakfast on the next day.

For the first time in several months, Jonathan Harker begins another diary (or journal). In the new journal, he writes that he is sure that Count Dracula has reached London; in fact, it was the Count whom he saw in Hyde Park. That day Jonathan meets Van Helsing, and the two discuss Jonathan's trip to Transylvania. Just before Van Helsing leaves, he notices an article in the local paper, and he becomes visibly shaken.

Dr. Seward also begins keeping a diary again, even though earlier he had resolved never to do so again. In his diary, Seward notes that Renfield is his same old self – that is, Renfield is back to counting flies and spiders. Seward notes that Arthur seems to be doing well and that Quincey Morris is with him. That very day, in fact, Van Helsing shows him the article in the paper concerning the Bloofer Lady. Van Helsing points out that the injuries to the children are similar to Lucy's neck injury; therefore, the incidents have something in common. Seward is skeptical that there is any connection between the injuries, but Van Helsing berates him, asking him, "Do you not think that there are things that you cannot understand and yet which are; that some people see things that others cannot?" Van Helsing continues to urge Seward to believe in things supernatural, to believe in things which, heretofore, he did not believe in. In desperation, Van Helsing finally tells Seward that the marks on the children "were made by Miss Lucy" (Chapter 15). For awhile, Seward has to struggle to master his anger against Van Helsing, and he questions the sanity of the good doctor. Van Helsing points out that he knows how difficult it is to believe something horrible, particularly about one so beloved as Lucy, but he offers to prove his accusation that very night.

The two men have a mutual acquaintance (Dr. Vincent), who is in charge of one of the children who was injured by the Bloofer Lady. They plan to visit the child and then to visit Lucy's grave.

The child is awake when Van Helsing and Seward arrive, and Dr. Vincent removes the bandages from around the child's neck, exposing the puncture wounds, which are identical to those which were on Lucy's throat. Dr. Vincent attributes the marks to some animal, perhaps a bat.

When they leave the hospital, it is already dark, and they go immediately to the cemetery and find the Westenra tomb. They enter the tomb and light a candle. To Seward's dismay, Van Helsing begins to open the coffin. Seward expects a rush of gas from the week-old corpse, but when the coffin is finally opened, they discover it to be empty.

Seward, despite what he sees, is not convinced; he believes a body-snatcher may have stolen the corpse. The two leave the tomb, and Van Helsing and Seward take up vigils in the cemetery near the Westenra tomb. After some hours, Seward sees "something like a white streak" and, then, at the same time, he sees something move near Van Helsing. When he approaches Van Helsing, he discovers that Van Helsing is holding a small child in his arms. Still, this is not proof enough for Seward. They take the child where a policeman will be sure to find it, and they then head home, planning to meet at noontime the next day.

The next day (September 27th), they return to the cemetery, and as soon as possible, they reenter the Westenra tomb and reopen the coffin again. To Seward's shock and dismay, there lies the lovely Lucy, "more radiantly beautiful than ever." Still, Seward is not convinced; again, he wonders if someone might not have placed her there, but he cannot understand why she looks so beautiful after being dead an entire week. Van Helsing then tells Seward that a horrible thing *must* be done: they must cut off Lucy's head, fill her mouth with garlic, and drive a stake through her heart. Yet before doing it, Van Helsing has second thoughts. He feels that he cannot perform the act without Arthur's and Quincey's knowing about it, since they both loved her and gave their blood for her.

That night, Van Helsing informs Seward that he intends to watch the Westenra tomb and try to prevent Lucy's prowling about by blocking the tomb's door with garlic and a crucifix. He leaves Seward a set of instructions which he is to follow if something should happen to him.

The following night (September 28th) Arthur and Quincey come to Van Helsing's room. After the two are convinced of Van Helsing's good intentions and have his trust, Van Helsing informs them of the things which he intends to do. First, he will open the coffin (which Arthur strongly objects to – until Van Helsing explains that Lucy might be one of the "Un-Dead"), then he will perform the necessary "service." Arthur, however, will not consent to *any* mutilation of Lucy's body. Van Helsing pleads that he *must* do these things for Lucy's sake, so that her soul will rest peacefully. A few hours later, the four men go to the cemetery. In the tomb, the coffin lid is removed, and they all see that the coffin is empty. Van Helsing asks for Seward's confirmation that the body was in the coffin yesterday; Seward, of course, concurs with Van Helsing. Van Helsing then begins an intricate ceremony: from his bag he removes a "thin, wafer-like biscuit" and crumbles it to a fine powder; then, he mixes the crumbs with a doughy substance and begins to roll the material into the crevices between the door jam and the mausoleum door. Van Helsing informs them that he is sealing the tomb so that the "Un-Dead may not enter." He informs them that the wafer was "the host" which he brought with him from Amsterdam. The four men hide among some trees near the tomb and begin waiting. Soon, by the light of the moon, the men see a ghostly white figure moving through the cemetery. As it nears them, it becomes all too apparent that the creature is, indeed, Lucy Westenra. According to Seward's diary entry, her "sweetness was turned to adamantine . . . and the purity to voluptuous wantonness." The four men surround her before the tomb. Lucy's lips are covered with fresh blood, and her burial gown is stained with blood. Upon learning that she is surrounded, Lucy reacts like a cornered animal. The child which she holds is tossed to the ground, and she moves towards Arthur saying, "Come, my husband, come." Arthur's love turns to hate and disgust, yet he is also petrified with fear. Just as Lucy is about to attack him, Van Helsing repels her with a crucifix. Dashing towards the tomb, she is prevented from entry by the host, which Van Helsing placed earlier around the door. Asking Arthur if he is to proceed with his duty, Arthur responds: "Do as you will. . . . There can be no horror ever any more." Advancing on the tomb, Van Helsing removes the seal around the door, and immediately, the ghostly body passes through the interstices and vanishes inside. After witnessing this, the men return home for a night's rest.

The next night (September 29th), the four men return to the Westenra tomb and perform the necessary ceremonies which destroy the vampire. Arthur himself must drive the stake through his finacée's heart. Before parting ways that evening, they vow to join together and seek out "the author of all this our sorrow" (Count Dracula) and destroy him.

Commentary

In these chapters, even though we have heard earlier that Jonathan Harker's journal was to be sealed as a bond of faith between Jonathan and Mina, we now discover that Mina has not only read it but transcribed it because Dr. Van Helsing thinks that something in it might provide a clue about the mystery of Lucy's death. Thus, as the novel began with Jonathan Harker's journal and then progressed for many chapters without his narration, now Mina and Harker are again both drawn back into the main story.

This novel has set the course for all subsequent vampire lore – for example, the belief that a wooden stake must be driven through the vampire's heart and that the head must be removed and the mouth stuffed with garlic. All of the numerous, subsequent treatments of the vampire legend depend on these factors. Furthermore, in Chapter 16, the term *nosferatu* is used. Stoker tells us that it is an Eastern European term and that it means the "Un-Dead"; this is the first time that all of the protagonists are privy to all of the information that Van Helsing has so far withheld. As a point of historical fact, *Nosferatu* is the title of two German films that deal with the Dracula legend (See the section on Filmography). Furthermore, the translation of "nosferatu" as the "Un-Dead" has now become standard usage.

It is interesting that the love which Arthur, Quincey, and Seward had for Lucy has been basely transfigured into hate at the sight of

Lucy; moreover, it is somewhat surprising that these lusty men are disgusted at the abundant sensuality of Lucy, now that she is a vampire. When she approaches Arthur in her vampire form, it is with a sensual embrace. Instead of arousing passion, however, there is only a feeling of repulsion and disgust. It is clear that in her vampire form, Lucy's *carnal* aspect is highlighted and emphasized. The ceremony which kills her "Un-Dead" self frees her pure spirit from the sinful, carnal nature of her body and is a rite of purification, as symbolized by the sudden return of *innocent* beauty to her face at the conclusion of the ceremony.

CHAPTERS 17-19

Summary

Dr. Seward's diary continues sometime later, and he details for us his first meeting with Mina Harker. Mina, he says, will travel with Seward to Seward's asylum, where she will stay as a guest. In *her* journal, Mina details the discussion which she and Seward had concerning Lucy's death. Mina agrees to type out Seward's diary, which has heretofore been kept on a phonograph. Seward is horror-struck that Mina may discover the true nature of Lucy's death, but Mina, through her persistence, convinces Seward to allow her to listen to the phonograph cylinders. Later, both Seward and Mina express their dismay at the stories which they read in each other's respective diaries.

The next day (September 30th), Jonathan arrives, and Seward expresses his admiration for Jonathan's courage. For the first time, Seward realizes that Count Dracula might be next door, at the estate at Carfax. Seward concludes his diary, noting that Renfield has been calm for several days. Seward assumes that Renfield's outbreak was due to Dracula's proximity.

Jonathan Harker discovers from his journey to Whitby that the "fifty cases of common earth" which arrived on Dracula's ship have been sent to the old chapel at Carfax. While Jonathan assumes that all fifty cases are still at Carfax, we later learn that Count Dracula has had them sent to various locations in and around London.

Mina is both pleased and inspired by the resolute, determined energy which she now sees in Jonathan; he now seems cured of his illness, full "of life and hope and determination." Later on the 30th,

Arthur Holmwood – now referred to as Lord Godalming – and Quincey Morris arrive. Lord Godalming is still physically shaken by the deaths of his father, Mrs. Westenra, and Lucy. Unable to restrain himself any longer, he breaks down and cries like a baby on Mina's breast.

In Chapter 18, Dr. Seward notes that Mina Harker wishes to see Renfield. He takes her to Renfield's room, and Renfield, curiously, asks them to wait until he tidies things up. "His method of tidying was peculiar. He simply swallowed all the flies and spiders in the boxes . . . ." Renfield is extremely polite to Mina and seems to respond in a most sane way to her inquiries. Van Helsing arrives and is pleased to discover that all the records – diaries, journals, etc. – are in order and that all those intimate with the Count now are to be presented with the facts surrounding the case.

Mina Harker, in her journal (September 30th), recalls in detail many of the things known about vampires, a subject which prior to this time she has been ignorant of. Van Helsing presents many conclusions about the *nosferatu* (or the "Un-Dead"): (1) They do not die; (2) can be as strong as twenty men; (3) can direct the elements – storms, fog, thunder, etc.; (4) can command the rat, the owl, the bat, the wolf, the fox, and the dog; (5) can grow large or become small at will; (6) can, at times, vanish and "become unknown"; and (7) can appear at will in different forms. The problem which the vampire's adversary must overcome is how to deal successfully with all of these obstacles. They all make a pact to work together in order to see how "the general powers arrayed against us can be controlled and to consider the limitations of the vampire." Van Helsing points out that the vampire has been known in all lands all over the world. From the world's information about vampires, it is known that: (1) the vampire cannot die due to the passing of time; (2) the vampire flourishes on the blood of human beings; (3) the vampire grows younger after feeding on blood; (4) its physical strength and vital faculties are refreshed by blood; (5) it cannot survive without blood; (6) it can survive for great lengths of time without any nourishment; (7) it throws no shadow; (8) it makes no reflection in a mirror; (9) it has the strength of many; (10) it can control wild packs of wolves and can become a wolf (as the Count did when his ship arrived at Whitby); (11) the vampire can transform itself into a bat; (12) it can appear in a mist, which it itself can create; (13) the vampire can travel on moonlight rays as elemental dust; (14) it can become so small and transparent that it can pass through the tiniest crevices; and (15) it can see perfectly in the dark. Its limitations are as follows: (1) it cannot enter a household unless it is summoned *first*; (2) its power ceases at daylight; (3) in whatever form it is in when daylight comes, it will remain in that form until sunset; (4) the vampire must always return to the unhallowed earth of its coffin, which *restores its strength* (this, of course, is the purpose of the fifty cases of earth); (5) garlic is abhorrent to a vampire; (6) the crucifix, holy water, and holy wafers (the host) are anathemas; (7) it is rendered inactive if a wild rose is placed over it; and (8) death occurs when a wooden stake is driven through the heart, the head cut off, and garlic stuffed in the mouth.

As Van Helsing concludes his lecture, Quincey Morris leaves the room, and a shot is heard outside. Morris explains that he saw a bat and fired at it.

On October 1st, early in the morning, Dr. Seward records that as they were about to leave the asylum, he received an urgent message from Renfield. The others ask if they may attend the meeting with Renfield, and they are astonished at the brilliance and lucidity of Renfield's plea to be released immediately. His scholarly logic and perfect elocution are that of a totally sane man. His request is denied.

In Chapter 19, in his journal, Jonathan Harker records that Seward believes Renfield's erratic behavior to be directly influenced by the immediate proximity of Count Dracula. Later, as they are about to enter Dracula's Carfax residence, Van Helsing distributes objects which will protect each of them from the vampire. The house, they discover, is musty, dusty, and malodorous. They immediately search out the chapel and, to their horror, they can find only twenty-nine of the original fifty boxes of earth. Suddenly, the chapel is filled by a mass of rats.

Towards noon, Seward records that Van Helsing is deeply fascinated by Renfield. On the same day, Mina feels strange to be left out of Jonathan's confidence, because she has no idea what happened last night, but she does remember that just before falling asleep, she heard unusual sounds and noises outside her window, and she felt as if she were in the grip of a strange lethargy. She thought that she saw a poor man "with some passionate entreaty on his part" who wanted inside. She put on her clothes, but she must have fallen asleep or gone into a trance, accompanied by strange dreams. When she awakened she noticed that the window of her bedroom was open, and she was certain that she closed it before she went to sleep. Things became confused in her mind, but she recalls seeing two red eyes which alarmed her extremely.

On the second of October, she records that she slept but felt very weak that day and asked for an opiate to help her sleep. The chapter closes as Mina feels sleep coming upon her.

Commentary

Chapter 17 is the first time in the novel when all of the protagonists are finally together. These six people – Mina, Jonathan, Dr. Van Helsing, Dr. Seward, Lord Godalming (Arthur), and Quincey Morris – will confront the evil represented by Count Dracula. They must undertake the task by themselves since no authority or outsider would possibly believe their story. These six people, of course, have positive proof of the existence of vampires. In fact, Jonathan feels rejuvenated in health now that he is confronting the evil Count head-on. Stoker is dependent on the tradition that only a few people are privy to information which exposes them to the dangerous forces of the supernatural, thus isolating them from the general populace. This is a standard device of many a thriller and gothic romance.

Chapter 18 is a key chapter of the novel, because for the first time Stoker defines the vampire and its supernatural powers, strengths, and the means by which the vampire can be entrapped. In all subsequent stories concerning vampires or Dracula himself, Stoker's parameters have been used – the garlic, the crucifix, the wooden stake, the holy wafers, etc. This chapter, then, defines the very essence of what constitutes vampire literature. Other authors may vary or slightly redefine these parameters, but the more traditional material concerning vampires is presented here.

The later portions of Chapter 19 present us with the first clue, however slight, that Mina Harker is to become the vampire's next victim. It is not by accident that he chooses Mina as his next victim; she is the wife of Jonathan Harker, whom the vampire encountered in Transylvania, and she was the closest friend of his last victim, Lucy Westenra. It is interesting that we are made aware of the Count's visit by the impressionistic writing of Mina herself. For example, she records things in her journal which she does not fully understand or associate with vampirism, but the reader, through dramatic irony, is fully aware of what is transpiring. There is a curious ambiguity presented in this chapter, as to how the vampire gains entrance to Mina's room. Recall that Van Helsing stated that vampires cannot enter a place without first being invited. The reader, at this point, does not have any idea as to how the vampire entered the room, unless it was because of the actions of Mina herself.

CHAPTERS 20-23

Summary

Jonathan, through his persistent investigations, discovers the whereabouts of twelve more of the boxes of earth: two groups of six were deposited at two different places in London. Jonathan assumes that it is the Count's plan to scatter the boxes throughout all of London. We should recall that there were twenty-nine boxes in the chapel and, added to the twelve which Jonathan discovered, they have now accounted for forty-one of the original fifty boxes. On the evening of October 2nd, Jonathan receives a note which informs him of the whereabouts of the remaining nine boxes. He also notes that Mina is lethargic and pale, but he puts it out of his mind.

That evening, all of the men meet to determine the course of action for retrieving the remaining nine boxes. Once again, Jonathan notes that Mina is very tired and pale.

Dr. Seward notes again that Renfield is remarkably lucid and, what is more, that Renfield seems to be a literate and learned man. Renfield scoffs at the notion of collecting flies and spiders. Later, however, Renfield reverts to his old ways. That night, Seward orders an attendant to stand guard outside Renfield's cell to note any aberrant behavior. Later that night there is a scream from Renfield's cell. Upon rushing to investigate, Seward discovers that Renfield has been seriously hurt – his face has been brutally beaten, there is a pool of blood on the cell floor, and his back is apparently broken.

Seward knows Renfield himself could not have administered the wounds to his own face – especially with his back broken. Dr. Van Helsing arrives, and they determine that Renfield is slipping fast; thus, they decide to operate immediately. Renfield, realizing that he is dying, tells them in an agony of despair what happened. Apparently, without identifying who it was, he says that *he* "came up to the window in the mist . . . but he was solid then . . . I wouldn't ask him to come in . . . ." He maintains that it was "he" who used to send the flies and spiders and the rats and dogs, promising that he would give Renfield everything that lives: ". . . all red blood, with years of life in it." Renfield refers to 'him' as "Lord and Master." Last night, Renfield says, "he" slid through the window. Renfield then says that after Mrs. Harker came to see him, he knew she wasn't the same and knew that "*he* had been taking the life out of her." Renfield tried to attack "him," but he was "burned," and his strength became "like water." Van Helsing realizes that "he is here and we know his purpose."

They rush to Mina's door immediately, leaving Renfield, and begin to arm themselves against the vampire. Van Helsing tries to open the door, which is locked, and when they finally break the door down, the sight which greets them is appalling. Jonathan Harker is lying unconscious on the bed and, kneeling on the edge of the bed, is the "white clad" Mina. Beside her is a tall thin man, clad in black – Count Dracula himself. His right hand is behind Mina's head, and he is forcing her to suck the blood from a cut in his bare chest. When the Count raises his head to greet them, his eyes are blood-red, his nostrils white, and they see "white sharp teeth, behind the full lips of the blood-dripping mouth, clamped together like those of a wild beast." The Count begins to attack them, but is repelled by the sacred wafer which is wielded as a weapon by Van Helsing. The lights go out, and when they come on again they see nothing but a faint vapor escaping under the door. Suddenly, Mina Harker recovers and emits an ear-piercing scream, filled with despair and disgust. Her face is "ghastly . . . from the blood which smeared her lips and cheeks and chin." From her throat trickles a thin stream of blood.

They have difficulty awakening Jonathan, and soon all traces of the vampire are lost. Mina feels unclean and untouchable. Lord Godalming examines the house and discovers that the Count has apparently destroyed all of their records and that Renfield is dead.

In spite of the horror that the story might cause, they ask Mina to recount the entire episode as best she can remember it. She recalls the first time she saw the thin, black clad man with the strange teeth when Lucy was alive, and how he subsequently came to her in her room and placed "his reeking lips" upon her throat. Mina would swoon and not know how long Dracula was overpowering her. He told her, "You are now to me flesh of my flesh . . . when my brain says 'Come,' you shall come." With that, he opened his shirt, and with a sharp nail he cut himself across his breast and pressed Mina's mouth to the wound, so that she either had to suffocate or drink the blood.

In Chapter 22, Jonathan Harker states that he feels compelled to either write in his journal or go mad after hearing Mina's story. Jonathan wants to stay with his wife, but since it is daylight, he knows that there is no danger to her. They go to Carfax and "sterilize" all of the boxes by placing a holy wafer within each of them. They then find a way to enter into the Count's most recent abode in Piccadilly (a prominent London square). Before they leave the asylum, they make sure that Mina is appropriately armed. As Van Helsing touches her forehead with a sacred wafer, Mina lets out a fearful scream because the wafer has seared and burned her forehead. Mina realizes that she is "unclean" and pleads with the men to kill her if she becomes a vampire.

Dracula's house in Piccadilly is as malodorous as the one at Carfax. Expecting to find nine boxes of earth, they are astonished to find only *eight* boxes. They do find keys to all of the other houses belonging to the Count, however, and then Quincey and Lord Godalming go off to destroy the boxes of earth in those houses.

Chapter 23 begins with Van Helsing, Harker, and Seward waiting for the return of Lord Godalming and Quincey Morris. Van Helsing, in an attempt to draw Jonathan's mind from Mina's condition, informs them of his resolution that Dracula must be killed, because, he says, Dracula is expanding his circle of power in order to harm innocent people; he cites Dracula's using Renfield to gain access to Mina. While waiting, they receive a note from Mina informing them that Dracula has left Carfax and is heading south, presumably to spend the evening in one of his other houses.

Lord Godalming and Quincey Morris return with the news that they have "sterilized" Dracula's remaining boxes, and Van Helsing suddenly realizes that Dracula will be forced to come to the house at Piccadilly soon. A short time later, they hear a key inserted into the door, and with a gigantic "panther-like" leap, Count Dracula enters and eludes their ambush. Through his diabolical quickness, the Count dodges their attempts to kill him, yet with a powerful thrust of a knife, Jonathan manages to rip open the Count's vestments, scattering banknotes and gold. As they corner the Count, he suddenly dodges away from them; then he retrieves a handful of money from the floor and throws himself out a window. As he flees, he taunts the men, reminding them that his revenge has just begun. All of them return to Seward's house, where Mina is awaiting them. Before they retire, Van Helsing prepares Mina's room against the vampire's entry.

In Jonathan Harker's journal, early on the morning of the 4th of October, he records how Mina asked him to call Van Helsing in order to hypnotize her. Under hypnosis, Mina is able to enter into the spirit of Dracula, and she becomes aware of flapping sails, the lapping of water, and the creaking of an anchor chain. Van Helsing concludes that Dracula is on board a ship that is now ready to sail. He now understands why Dracula so desperately tried to retrieve the gold coins – he needed ready cash to pay for his passage out of the country. Once again, they all renew their pledge to follow Dracula and destroy him.

Commentary

The two central incidents of these chapters involve Mina's encounter with Dracula and her coming under his evil influence. Second, these chapters are also concerned with the discovery and "sterilization" of the fifty boxes of earth which Dracula brought with him.

Since we earlier heard that a vampire can only enter an establishment if invited, we are at first surprised that he has been able to enter Mina's room, and we are inclined to wonder if *she* invited him in. Later, however, we learn that Dracula had used the "zoöphagous" patient Renfield to invite Dracula into the house. It is now clear why Stoker has been using the patient in the novel and also why all the principal characters are visitors in Seward's house. Later, Van Helsing uses the fate of Renfield to prove that Dracula is expanding his sphere of influence and is using innocent people to accomplish his aims – therefore, Dracula must be searched out and destroyed.

It becomes clear in these chapters that Dracula has some kind of mind control over his victims – that is, he can induce them to open windows, for example, in order to let him enter the home. Evidently Stoker was interested in hypnosis or "animal magnetism," since Van Helsing, through hypnotizing Mina, is able to learn of Dracula's whereabouts. Dracula, too, can hypnotize and, indeed, he is an individual of great personal magnetism. It is in these chapters that we learn that Stoker was, in fact, creating a gothic villain which would be similar to many gothic villains in earlier literature. Among other things, Count Dracula is a member of the corrupt aristocracy. The gothic villain/aristocrat was probably derived from Richardson's novels *Pamela* (1740) and *Clarissa* (1747), in which the villain's persecution of the innocent maiden dramatized for middle-class audiences the exaggerated nature of the class struggle.

It is important for the reader to understand the dramatic and philosophical importance of the villain's aristocratic heritage; if Dracula were a peasant, the story would hardly be as dramatic.

CHAPTERS 24 & 25

Summary

Van Helsing thinks that Jonathan Harker should stay in England with his wife, since he now knows that Dracula is returning to Transylvania. Jonathan Harker expresses in his journal how happy Mina is that Dracula is returning to Transylvania, but when Harker looks at the terrible mark on Mina's forehead (a sign of the evil "infection" that was caused by Dracula's blood), he is reminded of the reality of the vampire.

In her journal Mina Harker records the various reports concerning Dracula's departure. In the investigations, it was discovered that Dracula boarded a ship headed for Varna, a seaport on the Black Sea, near the mouth of the Danube River, the same place he had left from three months earlier. Evidently, Van Helsing has deduced the reason why Dracula came to England: Dracula's own country is so "barren of people" that he came to England, a place where life is rich and flourishing; he is now returning to his native soil to escape discovery.

Seward recalls his fear concerning Mina Harker, and in a short time, Van Helsing confirms his views: Mina is changing. Characteristics of the vampire are beginning to show in her face–that is, her teeth are longer, and her eyes are colder. He now fears that the Count could, by hypnosis, even over long distances, discover their plans, so they must keep Mina ignorant of their plans so that the Count cannot discover their whereabouts through her. They determine how long it will take the ship to reach Varna by sea, and they set a date for their own departure so that they will be in Varna before Count Dracula arrives. Then Mina surprises them by telling them that she should accompany them on the journey, since through hypnotizing her they can discover the whereabouts and intentions of Count Dracula. Everyone agrees with her, so it is settled: Mina will accompany them.

Chapter 25 begins with Dr. Seward's journal, written on the evening of October 11th. While Mina Harker is pleased that they are going to take her with them, she makes them repeat their promise *to kill her* if she is ever so totally changed into a vampire form that they cannot save her. All of them swear to do so, and Seward is pleased that the word "euthanasia" exists, because it euphemistically disguises the nature of her request. Mina makes one seemingly unusual request – in case she has to be killed, she would like to hear the "burial service" read to her immediately this very night.

Four days later, on the 15th of October, the six people arrive at Varna via the Orient Express, and when they arrive, they place Mina under hypnosis, during which she reports that she still senses the lapping of water against the ship. Van Helsing expresses his desire for them to board the ship as soon as it arrives at Varna. If they can board the ship before Dracula's coffin is removed, they will have him trapped, for one of the limitations of vampires is that they cannot cross running water. On the 17th, Jonathan notes in his journal that Van Helsing has secured admittance for the group to board Dracula's ship as soon as it arrives, so that they may more easily carry out the extermination of the vampire.

A week later, they receive a telegram from London reporting that the ship was sighted at the Dardanelles. Dr. Seward, therefore, assumes that it will arrive the next day. While waiting, Dr. Seward and Van Helsing are concerned about Mina's lethargy and her general state of weakness. They wait for two days and still the ship does not arrive. On the 28th of October they receive a telegram reporting that the ship has arrived at the port of Galatz, a city on the coast, near Varna.

Van Helsing offers a theory that when Mina was weak, the Count had pulled her spirit to him; now, the Count knows of their presence, as well as their efforts to trap and exterminate him. At present, however, Mina is feeling free and healthy, and she and Van Helsing use their knowledge of criminology to deduce that the Count is a "criminal type" – hence, he will act as a criminal, and therefore, his main purpose will be to escape his pursuers.

Commentary

It is only now, this late in the novel, that we learn the real reason why Dracula has come to England: his country is "barren of peoples," and England is teeming with numbers of new victims. Since Count Dracula brought with him fifty boxes of earth, one can assume that he was intending to stay in England quite some time.

The central incident of these chapters is the infection of Mina: she has a mark on her forehead, a sign that she is "unclean," that she is "infected" with vampirism. Her teeth have grown noticeably longer and her eyes have grown colder. We are also led to believe, in the course of these chapters, that the pursuers are in perfect control because they remember to arm themselves with all kinds of weapons – even Winchesters for the wolves. In theory, they will be able to track down Dracula's destination as far as Varna. However, in the next chapter, we discover that the Count deliberately misled them, and that instead of Varna, he had his box of earth sent on to Galatz, thus bypassing the awaiting pursuers.

The idea of hypnosis is continued throughout these chapters, as well as in the two remaining chapters, in order to track down Dracula, and once again Mina extracts a promise that if she begins to change into a vampire, she wants to be killed. In preparation she has the Church's burial service read to her. The notion of "euthanasia" would have been a shocking notion to Victorian readers.

CHAPTERS 26 & 27 and NOTE

Summary

On the 29th day of October, Dr. Seward records that Mina, under hypnosis, can hear and distinguish very little, and that the things which she does hear – such as the lowing of cattle – indicate that Dracula's coffin is now being moved up-river. Jonathan Harker records on October 30th that the captain of the ship which brought Dracula told of the unusual journey which they made from London to Galatz – that is, many of the Roumanians on board ship wanted him to throw the box overboard, but the captain felt obligated to deliver the box to the person to whom it was assigned. We find out, then, that one Immanuel Hildesheim received the box, and that the box was given to a Slovak, Petrof Skinsky. Skinsky was found dead in a churchyard, his throat apparently torn open by some wild animal. On that same day, Mina, having read all of the journal entries, and after consulting maps for waterways and roads, concludes that the Count would have had to take the river to Sereth, which is then joined to the Bristriza, which leads then to the Borgo Pass, where Jonathan Harker stopped at the beginning of the novel. They choose to separate and head for the pass: Van Helsing and Mina by train; Lord Godalming and Jonathan Harker by a steam launch (steamboat); Quincey Morris and Seward by horseback.

Harker and Godalming, in questioning various captains of other boats along the river, hear of a large launch with a double crew traveling ahead of them. They keep up the pursuit during the first three days of November. Meanwhile, Mina and Van Helsing arrive at Veresti on the 31st of October, where Van Helsing hires a horse and carriage for the last seventy miles of the journey.

Chapter 27 begins with a continuation of Mina Harker's journal. She records that she and Van Helsing traveled all day by carriage on the first of November. She remarks that she thinks the countryside is beautiful, yet the people are "very, very superstitious." In one house where the two of them stop, a woman noticed the red mark on Mina's forehead and crossed herself and pointed two fingers at Mina "to keep off the evil eye." That evening, Van Helsing hypnotizes Mina, and they learn that Dracula is still on board ship. On the 2nd of November, they again travel all day towards the Borgo Pass, hoping to arrive on the morning of the 3rd of November. They arrive at the Borgo Pass, and Van Helsing again hypnotizes Mina. They discover that the Count is still on board ship; after Mina awakens from the trance, she is full of energy and zeal, and she miraculously knows the way towards the Count's castle; she also "knows" the location of an unused side road, a road which is unmarked. They choose to take that path. That day Mina sleeps considerably and seems incredibly weak and lethargic. When Van Helsing attempts to hypnotize her again, he discovers that he can no longer do it. He has lost his power to hypnotize.

They spend the night in a wild forest east of the Borgo Pass, and Van Helsing builds a fire. Then, using a holy wafer, he places Mina in a protective circle. Later that night, the three female vampires which accosted Jonathan materialize near their campfire and tempt Van Helsing with their teeming sexuality. They also tempt Mina to come with them. The horses evidently die of terror, and Van Helsing's only weapon against the three female vampires is the fire and the holy wafer. At dawn, the sunlight drives away the three female vampires.

On the afternoon of the 5th of November, Van Helsing and Mina arrive by foot at Count Dracula's castle. Using a heavy blacksmith's hammer, Van Helsing knocks the castle door off its hinges and enters Dracula's demesnes. Recalling the description in Jonathan's journal, Van Helsing finds his way to the old chapel where Dracula lies during his non-active times. In his search of the old chapel, Van Helsing discovers the three graves of the three female vampires. He performs the purification ritual and puts an end to the female vampires. The female vampires' voluptuous beauty dissolves into dust upon the driving of a stake through their hearts. Van Helsing then finds a large tomb "more lordly than all the rest," upon which is one word: DRACULA. Van Helsing crushes a holy wafer and lays it within the tomb "and so vanished him from it, Un-Dead, forever." Before he leaves the castle, Van Helsing places holy material around the entrance so that the Count can never enter the castle again.

The novel ends with a passage from Mina Harker's journal, an entry that begins on the late afternoon of the 6th of November, a date some six months since the novel began. Mina and Van Helsing are on foot, traveling east in the midst of a heavy snowfall. The howling of wolves seems perilously close. On a high mountain road, utilizing his field glasses, Van Helsing notices in the distance a group of men; they seem to be gypsies around a cart. Van Helsing knows instinctively that the cart is carrying a box of un-holy dirt containing the Count and that they must reach the box before sunset, which is quickly approaching. The two men who are riding toward the North, Van Helsing assumes, must be Quincey Morris and Dr. Seward. This would mean that from the other direction, Jonathan and Lord Godalming must not be far away. Simultaneously, the six people converge on the wagon and the gypsies. The sun continues to set.

Jonathan and Lord Godalming stop the gypsies by using their Winchesters, just as Morris and Seward arrive, wielding their guns. With an almost superhuman effort, Jonathan eludes the defenders, leaps upon the cart, and throws the box to the ground. Quincey, wielding his knife, slashes his way through the gypsies and gains access to the box, but not before he is stabbed by one of the gypsies. Regardless of the wounds, Quincey, along with Jonathan, rips the lid from the box. Inside is the dreaded Count Dracula, covered with the un-holy dirt which has been jostled all over him. As the six of them stare into the coffin, Dracula's eyes look toward the setting sun, "and the look of hate in them turned to triumph." Then, at the very last moment of sunlight, Jonathan, wielding a great knife, chops off Count Dracula's head, while Quincey Morris's bowie knife plunges into the Count's heart, "and almost in the drawing of a breath," writes Mina, "the whole body crumbled into dust and passed from sight." Mina notices that even at the moment of death, within such a horrid face and image, she sees a look of peace. The gypsies, seeing the body disintegrate, withdraw in abject fright. Sadly, Quincey Morris has been fatally wounded; before he dies, however, he is able to note that the curse on Mina's forehead is gone. Quincey dies "a gallant gentleman."

In a Note attached to the end of the novel (reportedly from Jonathan Harker), we learn that it is seven years later; he and Mina have a son whom they named Quincey. Lord Godalming and Dr. Seward are both happily married. In a final note of irony, Jonathan reports that of all the material of which "the record" is made, "there is hardly one authentic document"; the only remaining notes are those which have been transcribed on a typewriter: "Therefore, we could hardly ask anyone . . . to accept these as proofs of so wild a story."

Commentary

The closing chapters of the novel suggest a type of chase novel, with the "good guys" chasing the evil person, who seems to be able to constantly elude them. Even at the end of the novel, it seems as though the Count will escape into the sinking sunset before the "rituals" can be performed upon him. Actually, for most readers, the last half of the novel becomes somewhat long and drawn out, but this novel was written at the end of the Victorian period when the reading public expected novels to last a long time. The killing of Dracula, of course, represents the social victory of middle-class morality over the corrupt morality of the aristocracy. The latent virtue of the Count is revealed in Mina's account, however, for as the Count is freed from the influence of the vampire form, his face contains a look of peace.

That the events really happened is now questioned by the final Note, which announces that all of the original documents have been lost and what we have read has been no more than the typewritten, transcribed notes of the originals, notes which cannot be used as absolute proof of the horrible things which have transpired.

In spite of the flaws of this novel, it has been an unlimited source of stories, plays, novels, and movies, as well as a source for assorted psychological theories. This novel is an example of a type of literature in which the germ, or kernel, idea far transcends the execution.

THE AMERICAN HORROR FILM AND THE INFLUENCE OF GERMAN EXPRESSIONISM

What exactly is a "horror film," or, more specifically, what exactly is *horror*? In what ways are our expectations different when we go to see a horror film than when we go to see a "western film" or a "science fiction film"? What is it that we hope to experience when we go to see a "horror film"?

Certainly, we expect to be "terrified," whatever that may be, or at least we are prepared to be "frightened" in some way; we expect the hair to rise on the back of our necks. But what is it that terrifies us, or "frightens" us, or, essentially, incites in us a sense of *horror*? Is it the presence of "horrible creatures"–however we may imagine them? Or is it the presence of ghosts, or other kinds of supernatural creatures, that frightens us? Certainly, the supernatural is present in all these experiences, and human beings generally fear the supernatural because things supernatural are considered hostile to human life. The fact that human beings fear the supernatural can be observed every Sunday; priests and ministers, for example, often exhort us to *fear* God. Yet God, ideally, is *not* hostile to human life.

Thus, some consideration of what horror is may help us to arrive at some tentative conclusion about the nature of horror. Tentatively, perhaps we can consider what horror does: *horror reaffirms the sacred, or Holy, through a formulaic plot in which human beings encounter the demonic, or Un-Holy.* If there *are* Un-Holy beings, by implication, there are Holy beings. To test this tentative hypothesis, perhaps an application of it to classic horror stories would be helpful.

This hypothesis is certainly applicable to *Dracula*. The Count has a terrifying sense of the demonic about him, suggested superficially by his appearance. Yet *religious* artifacts such as the cross affect the Count (in fact, it has become a popular cultural cliche that to ward off a vampire, all one has to do is brandish a cross – even if the "cross" is no more than crossed forefingers).

Horror has an interesting history. Essentially, the Cthulhu Mythos of H. P. Lovecraft posits the existence of a race of supernatural beings which are hostile to human life, eagerly awaiting their chance to reclaim the earth and rid it of human beings. Lovecraft, especially in such stories as "The Colour Out of Space," "The Shadow over Innsmouth," and "The Rats in the Walls," was perhaps the first Western author to write exclusively in the horror genre, and he quickly learned how to manipulate the intuitive revulsion that human beings have towards tentacled and clawed creatures. And, in addition, Lovecraft's creatures, besides being hideously and abnormally ugly, *reek* horribly.

Of course, there are other works of horror which do not precisely conform to the tentative definition of horror, such as Robert Louis Stevenson's *Dr. Jekyll and Mr. Hyde* or Joseph Conrad's *Heart of Darkness*. Yet what these works posit is that if there *is* anything demonic or Un-Holy that exists, it consists of those obscure motivations and desires which lurk within the *human mind*. These works conform to what we can label "modern horror," as opposed to "classic horror."

Concerning "classic horror," one of the first great horror films, *The Cabinet of Dr. Caligari* (1919), certainly subscribes to the "modern horror" genre also. What is ostensibly a tale of insane authority becomes the musings of a madman. In fact, the influence of German Expressionism on Hollywood films of the Thirties and Forties was tremendous. As an art form, Expressionism is generally considered to be best represented by the works of Van Gogh, Cézanne, and Edward Munch. In painting, Expressionistic art is characterized by a sense of imbalance in the pictorial arrangements in order to achieve distortion; the use of oblique angles and sharp curves; a distortion of line and color, where primary colors are generally used in violent contrast; and a subjective vision of the exterior world. Expressionism also usually incorporates the style of *grisaille*, painting in grey monotone in which objects are often seen only with a suggestion of form and outline without attention to precise detail. The content of Expressionistic art is characterized by its grotesqueness and implausibility. It is a revolt against both Naturalism and Impressionism and has similar counterparts in literature and sculpture.

The enormously creative German cinema in the 1920s was influenced, on the one hand, by the theater of Max Reinhardt, an innovative stage director, and, on the other, it was influenced by Expressionistic art. The advances in lighting techniques, pioneered by Reinhardt, coupled with the rise of Expressionism, was of supreme importance to the experimental film-makers in post World War I Germany. Most of the actors in the early Expressionistic films were members of Reinhardt's acting company; later, some of them became film directors themselves.

The first great Expressionistic masterpiece in film is *The Cabinet of Dr. Caligari* (1919), written by Hans Janowitz and Carl Mayer, and directed by Robert Wiene. Janowitz was deeply impressed by the work of Paul Wegener, a member of Reinhardt's acting troupe, who had directed the influential *Student of Prague* (1913), in collaboration with the Dane Stellan Rye, and *The Golem* (1915), remade in 1920.

Many of the Expressionistic film-makers in Germany during the Twenties eventually came to the United States. *Caligari* screenwriter Carl Mayer did, as well as Conrad Veidt, the actor who played the somnambulist Cesare in *Caligari*. (Veidt, interestingly enough, was also a member of Reinhardt's acting company.) In addition to these men, the great German film director F. W. Murnau, who directed the first "vampire" film, *Nosferatu* (1922), also went to Hollywood and directed several important films. The innovative Expressionistic cinematographer Karl Freund, who had photographed Wegener's 1920 version of *The Golem* and Fritz Lang's science-fiction classic, *Metropolis* (1927), became one of the most in-demand cinematographers in Hollywood. Freund was the cinematographer of *Dracula* (1931), and he also became an accomplished film director. He directed such horror film masterpieces as *The Mummy* (1932, the first of the series) and *Mad Love* (1934). *Mad Love* starred the now famous, late actor Peter Lorre, who achieved stardom with his powerful portrayal of the child murderer in Fritz Lang's *M* (1931). Fritz Lang, director of *Metropolis* (1927), was the first scheduled director of *The Cabinet of Dr. Caligari*, but he was committed to finish an earlier project. The Expressionist Paul Leni, a set designer for Max Reinhardt, came to the United States in 1927 and directed Conrad Veidt in *The Man Who Laughs* (1928), a silent film produced by Universal Pictures. Leni is important because he singlehandedly developed a new genre of the horror film, juxtaposing scenes which utilized carefully designed and lighted sets and uniquely focused cameras against scenes intended as comic interludes. Leni's unique approach was certainly an influence on James Whale, the director of the first two *Frankenstein* films. Leni's influence can also be found in the work of Whale's art director for the first two Universal *Frankenstein* pictures – Charles D. Hall, who was the art director for Leni's *The Man Who Laughs* (1928), *The Cat and the Canary* (1927), and *The Last Warning* (1929). Although Leni's output was slight (he died in Hollywood in 1929), he was an important link between the German and American cinemas.

Thus, the influence of German Expressionism on early Hollywood films is profound and readily evident. Most directors truly concerned about film art knew of the German Expressionistic films and learned from them. Upon close examination of the classic horror films of the Thirties, it is discovered that these films are not simply idle "crowd-pleasers," but serious attempts by concerned individuals at producing art.

FILMS INFLUENTIAL ON THE PRODUCTION OF *DRACULA* FILMS

The following selected filmography does not attempt to be, nor does it wish to be, exhaustive or complete. Nevertheless, the listing does present the more interesting and noteworthy "vampire" films. Every attempt has been made to include those films which possibly can be seen by contemporary audiences. Unfortunately, some films have disappeared or have been lost; therefore, no attempt has been made to include those films. In addition, most foreign productions have been excluded. Of the foreign productions, only those films which possibly can be seen by American audiences have been included. The notes and annotations on the films produced by Hammer Studios of Great Britain are dependent largely on *A Heritage of Horror: The English Gothic Cinema 1946-72*, by David Pirie (London: Gordon Fraser, 1973).

SELECTED FILMOGRAPHY

Rating Scale

***** A film that is a "must-see"; both artistically brilliant and influential in the history of cinema.

**** An excellent film, distinguished by its innovation on the genre because of its technical brilliance, yet artistically insubstantial in some way.

*** A good film, which, due either to negligence in production or to technical incompetence, resulted in no special distinction; most likely, a work which is exploitive of the genre; nevertheless, a film that is valuable.

** Mediocre. Technically competent, nostalgically interesting, yet it carries no special distinction whatsoever.

* Poor. A film in which, in addition to the producer's irresponsibility, the directorial integrity is in question.

Nosferatu (or, A Symphony of Horror) (1922). ***** Directed by the acclaimed German Expressionist F. W. Murnau and photographed by the brilliant Fritz Arno Wagner (*M*), this is one of the most critically acclaimed horror films. Max Schreck's appearance in the film is perhaps one of the most memorable in all of cinema history: pale and thin, his version of a vampire has a shaved head with two elongated front teeth, sunken cheeks, wide bulging eyes, and fingernails which are extremely long, curved, and pointed like claws. Because Murnau did not have the literary rights to Bram Stoker's *Dracula*, he changed the setting, altered the plot slightly and changed the vampire's name to Count Orlock. *Nosferatu* can be considered the first vampire film in much the same way that Stoker's *Dracula* is the first vampire novel; every subsequent artistic attempt must measure itself against both this film and the novel.

London After Midnight (1927) *** This silent film was directed by Tod Browning (who would eventually direct *Dracula* for Universal). It starred Lon Chaney as Inspector Edmund Burke, alias "Mooney," a fake vampire. The story was based on Browning's own novel, entitled *The Hypnotist*. *London After Midnight* may be, in fact, the first full-length American vampire film. Murnau's *Nosferatu* did not reach the United States until 1929, when it was released as *Nosferatu, the Vampire*. Curiously, Chaney's make-up is similar, though not identical, to Max Schreck's in *Nosferatu*.

Dracula (1931) * * * Directed by the "Edgar Allan Poe of the Cinema," Tod Browning, and photographed by the Expressionist cinematographer Karl Freund, this film is the first vampire *sound* film and is still one of the most popular vampire films. Its popularity is probably due to Bela Lugosi's Dracula, who, with his authentic Hungarian accent and satanic appearance, captured the popular culture's imagination as an authentic vampire. The script for the film was not based on Stoker's *Dracula*, however. Instead, it was based on a popular play by John Balderston and Hamilton Deane. Lugosi, in fact, recreated his stage role for the movie. While this original movie is a popular film, it is not a great film. Browning's direction is adequate but not compelling; it does not match the energy of his earlier films – such as *The Unholy Three* (1925), or *The Unknown* (1927), which are more lavish and carefully directed; nor does it approach the genuinely grotesque horror of his next film, *Freaks* (1932). Freund's photography is rather lackluster; his next effort, *Murders in the Rue Morgue* (1932), made with Robert Florey, is a more appropriate example of Freund's innovative technique. Still, *Dracula*, like the novel, has managed to capture the public's imagination ever since its release.

Vampyr (1932) * * * * * This film is one of Carl Theodore Dreyer's best movies, a film which relies on suggested rather than visible horror. It has a remarkably gloomy sense of atmosphere; every shot is as carefully composed as the finest photograph. It is probably one of the most artistically crafted of any vampire film, perhaps of all horror films – with the exception of *The Cabinet of Dr. Caligari* (1919) and *Nosferatu* (1922).

The Vampire Bat (1933). * * A rather run-of-the-mill horror picture which has a superb cast: Lionel Atwill, Fay Wray, and Dwight Frye (who played the role of Renfield in Browning's *Dracula*, as well as the hunchbacked laboratory assistant of Dr. Frankenstein in *Frankenstein* (1931). The story takes place in a remote Balkan village, where a "mad" doctor tries to conceal his bizarre experiments by creating a vampire "scare."

The Mark of the Vampire (1935). * * * Made in 1935, but not released until 1972, the film is a re-make by Tod Browning of his earlier silent film *London After Midnight*. Browning expanded the original story by adding a seductive female ghoul (played by Carol Borland). The movie is memorable because it was the last of Tod Browning's horror films – four years later, in 1939, Browning retired from filmmaking altogether.

Dracula's Daughter (1936). ** This film was directed by Lambert Hillyer for Universal. Hillyer was a prolific director, responsible for directing dozens of "B-grade" westerns. The story is based on a short story by Bram Stoker entitled "Dracula's Ghost," which was originally part of *Dracula*, but extracted just before the novel's release. Thus, one can see how derivative vampire films were becoming. The direction was increasingly hackneyed, and the writers were desperately lacking in inspiration. Universal did the same thing with the *Frankenstein* series; they produced countless spin-offs of the original, and each subsequent film was representative of uninspired artistic conviction.

The Vampire Bat (1940). ** In this film, vampire bats are bred for instruments of revenge by a "mad" scientist (Bela Lugosi). A rather uninspired film which exploited both the audience's attraction to vampirism and Lugosi's cult personality.

Spooks Run Wild (1941). * Another film which exploits the cult of personality surrounding Lugosi; in this case, he plays Nardo, a magician suspected of being a vampire. It is a rather shoddy attempt to adapt the plot of *The Cabinet of Dr. Caligari* to a vampire story.

Son of Dracula (1943). * Written by Curt Siodmak (creator of the original script for *The Wolf Man* (1941), a true classic of the horror film genre), the premise is hardly original. It is, basically, the plot of *Dracula* all over again: the son of the Count emigrates to England in search of new victims, except that his name isn't Dracula, but, instead, it is Alucard – Dracula spelled backwards. This kind of comic book gimmick is indicative of the inspiration for this banal film. Moreover, casting Lon Chaney, Jr., an actor capable of eliciting a great deal of sympathy for his (often) confused and misunderstood 'Beastman' was a serious mistake.

Return of the Vampire (1943). * The plot of *Dracula* again, except adapted to World War II England. Instead of searching for new victims, the screenwriters suggest that the vampire (named Armand Tesla) is in England seeking revenge against those who tried to kill him.

House of Frankenstein (1944). * As the popularity of the *Frankenstein* series declined, Universal (which produced every American *Frankenstein* picture until 1948) attempted to capture an audience by tossing into the plot every "monster" popular at the time – the Wolf Man, Dracula, Frankenstein, and even the ever-present "mad" scientist. A predictably silly and banal film.

House of Dracula (1945). *** Directed by Erle C. Kenton, *House of Dracula* contains an acting performance by Onslow Stevens (as Dr. Edelmann) which approaches the sublimity of Ernest Thesiger's in *The Bride of Frankenstein* (1935), possibly the best horror film ever made. Edelmann discovers the Frankenstein monster and is prompted to revive it, but is convinced by his beautiful, yet hunchbacked laboratory assistant (played by Jane Adams) to forsake his attempt to revive the monster. Eventually, Edelmann, who has become infected by a vampire's blood, chooses to revive the monster. The material, however, is never quite under control by director Kenton; the film stumbles and plods along at its own unique pace, while the preposterousness of the action proves to be the very reason why the film works. Despite its B-movie status and its illogical plotting, the film is ultimately both humane and moral.

Isle of the Dead (1945). * This RKO-Radio production, directed by Mark Robson and produced by the phenomenal "boy wonder" producer Val Lewton, promises much and produces almost nothing. The story centers around a group of people stranded on an island and menaced by a malevolent force, and the situation seems insolvable. In other words, the plot is as banal as an exhausted horror genre can make it. When plague breaks out among the group, an old peasant woman suspects the presence of "vorvolakas," demons which "drain all the life and joy from

from those who want to live." *Isle of the Dead* is essentially a poorly done "stalk and slash" movie and has no vampire *per se*.

The Vampire's Ghost (1945). * * * A film notable for the script and story by Leigh Brackett (1915-78), one of the best of the American screenwriters (she wrote the script for Howard Hawks's *The Big Sleep* (1946) along with William Faulkner and Jules Furthman, as well as the screenplay for Robert Altman's *The Long Goodbye* (1973), among others). The film has a disturbingly oppressive atmosphere and concerns a vampire terrorizing a small African village.

The Thing (1951). * * *The Thing* is memorable for several reasons: as a piece of popular culture trivia (James Arness was ' The Thing'; as the first science fiction film which utilizes the vampire figure; and as one of the few science fiction films of which critics are fond). Yet, *The Thing* neither merits the lavish critical acclaim it has received, nor does it truly deserve to be forgotten. The plot of *The Thing* is stereotypical horror: a group of victims are stranded and isolated in a remote location and are stalked by a hostile presence.

Plan Nine from Outer Space (1966). * A 1-star rating for this film was given reluctantly. The film is so badly done that it must be seen to be believed. Its alternative title gives one a clue to its plot: *Grave Robbers from Outer Space*. It is Bela Lugosi's last film. In fact, Lugosi died during production of the film, and he was replaced by a look-alike who always kept his cape up around his face so that the audience (presumably) wouldn't know that the actor wasn't Lugosi. Essentially, the plot concerns a group of aliens from outer space who intend to implement "Plan Nine"–the revival of corpses which will be used as troops against living human beings.

The Horror of Dracula (1957). * * * * * This is the first of Great Britain's Hammer Studios' vampire films, and it is a true classic of the genre. It was directed by Terence Fischer and was written by Jimmy Sangster, who based the film on Stoker's novel.

Sangster managed to return the Count to the tradition of the English gothic villain: he is a charming and intelligent aristocrat who transforms his female victims into carnal, lascivious creatures. The death of the Count is similar to the death of the vampire in Murnau's *Nosferatu*: he is tricked into staying out until daybreak, and then he is exposed to sunlight, which causes him to crumble away into dust. Not only does the villain's demise allow special effects, but it culminates the hero's ritualistic chase of the villain to his castle.

Blood of the Vampire (1957). *** An interesting film which revolves around a prison warden who is also a vampire and supplies himself with blood from his prisoners. Prints of this film are rare.

The Brides of Dracula (1960) **** *Brides* was Hammer's sequel to *The Horror of Dracula*, and it features the same writer and director as the previous effort. This film also has a climactic chase scene and a sufficiently bombastic demise of the vampire.

Black Sunday (1960). **** Based on a short story by Nikolai Gogol entitled "The Viy," *Black Sunday* (also known as *Revenge of the Vampire*) was labeled by critic Carlos Clemens as a "relentless nightmare," and it has been said of cinematographer Ubaldo Terzoni's photography that it was "the best black and white photography to enhance a horror movie in the past two decades." Directed by Mario Bava, the film depicts a witch/vampire's vengeance on the descendants of the people who ritualistically killed her in the seventeenth century. Virtually unknown outside of the horror film, the film stars Barbara Steele, who has become, curiously, a cult figure.

Kiss of the Vampire (1962). *** Hammer Studios eventually found it difficult to continue resurrecting the Count, but this film, directed by Don Sharp, features a clever script about a young couple seduced into depravity while on their honeymoon in Bavaria.

Devils of Darkness (1964). * * Interesting only as trivia, this was the first of the British vampire films in a modern setting—that of "swinging London."

The Last Man on Earth (1964). * * * Based on Richard Matheson's classic science fiction novel *I Am Legend,* in which the sole survivor of a horrible plague is a man who wanders around in a grim, deserted world and is relentlessly stalked at night by a group of vampires. Shot in black and white, the film is quite unrelenting in its vision of terror. Vincent Price plays the title role. The story was later re-made in the United States (this production was Italian), and it was entitled *The Omega Man* (1971).

Dracula—Prince of Darkness (1965). * * * * Directed by veteran director Terence Fischer, this film is a true gem of the vampire cinema. A group of bored and provincial Victorian couples are stranded in a remote castle, where a lone, devoted follower of the Count murders one of them and uses the victim's blood to resurrect the Count by pouring it over his ashes. Unfortunately, the Count had degenerated into a one-dimensional character: he is just menacing; no longer is he charming or refined or even rapaciously seductive. The Van Helsing figure in the novel is replaced in this film by a priest—Father Sandor, who stalks the vampire to his castle and brings about his demise.

Billy the Kid vs. Dracula (1966). * Perhaps the worst horror film—if one can call it that—ever made, along with *Jesse James Meets Frankenstein's Daughter* (1965); both were directed by William Beaudine. The most amazing thing about this film is why—and how—it ever got produced.

The Fearless Vampire Killers (1967). * * * This is Roman Polanski's much over-praised vampire film, an attempt to parody the genre, a task easily enough accomplished given the trivialized state of the contemporary genre. At least, however, Polanski got the mythology right, but the humor is rather juvenile, and his attempts at eroticism are adolescent.

A Taste of Blood (1967). * * A run-of-the-mill horror film about an American who is infected with the vampire blood of one of his ancestors. Its form is that of the "stalk and slash" movie – the absolute bottom-of-the-barrel stereotypical formula.

Dracula Has Risen from the Grave (1968). * * A Hammer Studios' film in which, as the title implies, the plot is banal and the writer's inspiration is sorely lacking.

Taste the Blood of Dracula (1970). * * * * Hammer Studios hired Hungarian-born Peter Sasdy to direct this sequel to 1968's *Dracula Has Risen from the Grave*, using a script by John Elder (Anthony Hinds). Coupled with Arthur Grant's superb photography, Hammer achieved its best effort since 1957's *Horror of Dracula*. In this picture, the Dracula presence is explicitly associated with the disintegration of the family, coming much closer in spirit to Stoker's novel. Certainly one of the best vampire films Hammer ever made.

The Scars of Dracula (1970). * Produced immediately after *Taste the Blood of Dracula* and directed by Roy Ward Baker, this film is one of the most seriously flawed vampire films which Hammer ever attempted. A vicious, unbelievably cruel film.

Count Yorga, Vampire (1970). * * Directed by Bob Kelljan, this production features a vampire in the tradition of the English gothic villain. Courteous and refined, Count Yorga seeks the blood of Southern California teenage girls. Unfortunately, the situations have become stereotyped, and the plot is absolutely predictable.

Daughters of Darkness (1970). * Harry Kümel's film is concerned with the sexuality of vampirism. This film features bisexual female vampires and lots of self-consciously "arty" scenes composed of red, black, and white colors. This kind of sophomoric symbolism is indicative of the artistic pretensions of this silly little soft-core film. The film did well, however, when it premiered in the United States in May of 1971.

House of Dark Shadows (1970). *Another of the bumper crop of vampire films made in 1970 which exploits the teenage fascination with *Dark Shadows*, a gothic soap opera of the late '60's. The vampire in this film and in the TV series was played by Jonathan Frid.

The 'Karnstein Trilogy': *The Vampire Lovers* (1970) ** directed by Roy Ward Baker; *Lust for a Vampire* (1970) **½ directed by Jimmy Sangster; and *Countess Dracula* (1970) ** directed by Peter Sasdy. These films are based on Joseph Sheridan Le Fanu's short story "Carmilla" (1871), a story of vampirism with lesbian overtones. Thus, these films exploit the sexuality of vampirism – specifically, a female vampire whose favorite victims are the daughters of nobility. Most of the action of these films centers around Karnstein castle. All of the films feature wonderfully stylized sets and (self-consciously) "arty" photography, creating a rather dream-like atmosphere. *The Vampire Lovers*, the first of the series, was a huge commercial success, and thus inspired Hammer to produce more of the same. The second film, *Lust for a Vampire*, is probably the best of the trilogy, although it too exults in lots of free-flowing blood. *Countess Dracula* features a vampire who bathes in the blood of her victims in order to restore her youth and beauty. All of these films are blatant "soft-core" pornography and were extremely popular with American teenage audiences.

The Omega Man (1971). *** A competent film adaptation of Matheson's *I Am Legend* (see *The Last Man on Earth*, 1964) starring Charleton Heston in the title role. This film has rather stylized production values, though its symbols – such as that of Heston's crucifixion at the end of the film – is rather blatant and heavy-handed. Nevertheless, a thoroughly competent and delightful film.

Twins of Evil (1971). ** This film was a further attempt by Hammer Studios to exploit Le Fanu's "Carmilla," with predictable results.

Dracula, A.D. 1972 (1971) * and **Dracula Is Dead (1972).** * Both of these films were directed by Alan Gibson and scripted by Don Houghton. The second of the above films is a sequel to the first. These films represent Hammer's attempt to set the story of Dracula in modern London. The results are wretched. In both films, Christopher Lee played the vampire while Peter Cushing played the protagonist.

Vampire Circus (1971). *** Directed by Robert Young, this film is one of Hammer's plethora of films during the 1970-71 period which have any merit at all and is well worth seeing.

The Return of Count Yorga (1971). **** With the aid of Yvonne Wilder on the script, who also plays a featured role in the film as a Cassandra-like mute, Bob Kelljan was able to surpass his mediocre *Count Yorga, Vampire* and create something close to a classic of the genre – albeit, for the most part, forgotten. With the aid of cinematographer Bill Butler (*Jaws, One Flew Over the Cuckoo's Nest*), Kelljan was able to create a film with an overpowering sense of menace and pervasive horror. The presence of the vampire is similar to Stoker's – an indication of growing social disruption. Count Yorga and followers completely disrupt an orphanage and pervert all relationships. The ending of the film is one of the best of the vampire cinema. Butler unleashed his visual pyrotechnics; it was filmed in slow motion freeze frame for optimum effect.

Blacula (1973). *** Shakespearian actor William Marshall played the role of the vampire in this picture, which is neither one of the great vampire films nor a "blackploitation" film. The film has a spirit of fun which wasn't present in any vampire films of the previous decade.

Scream, Blacula, Scream (1973). ** Director Bob Kelljan was not able to achieve the merits of the original *Blacula* (directed by William Crain), much less approach the artistry of his best film, *The Return of Count Yorga,* with this picture.

Andy Warhol's Dracula (1975). **** Released a few months after *Andy Warhol's Frankenstein* (May, 1974), this film, like its predecessor, evaluates its particular genre, in this case the vampire cinema, and it views it as one which exploits the subliminal psycho-sexual fears of its audience. Of course, the assumption of the film-makers is that these audiences are awaiting some kind of ludicrous confirmation of those subliminal fears through ritual enactment and formulaic plot. Thus, the proceedings of *Andy Warhol's Dracula* are predictably ludicrous and necessarily silly. They are also, paradoxically, quite disturbing.

Old Dracula (1975). * An American International release – in the worst sense of that infamous genre. This film, which stars David Niven as the vampire, is a prolonged practical joke at the audience's expense.

Dracula (1979). ** Directed by John Badham (*Saturday Night Fever*), this production attempts to be quite stylized and original. The script is based on a popular Broadway play of the same title, and Frank Langella re-created his stage role for the film. The film focuses on Dracula's seductive charms, and it features him as an archetypal Byronic lover. The premise is not so clever (or original) as the film-makers thought. The plot is predictably stereotyped.

Nosferatu (1979). ** The nature of this film is the natural result when a world-acclaimed artistic director sees fit to give his stamp of approval to a genre which has undergone pop culture trivializing. This is Werner Herzog's re-make (called homage by the director) of Murnau's classic. The film was, predictably, self-consciously "arty" and did not transcend the genre to any large degree whatsoever.

Love at First Bite (1980). ** Premise: Dracula is kicked out of his Transylvanian castle by local officials and comes to America, where he falls in love (with a beautiful woman) for the first time in his life. As a Dracula "spoof," it exhibits some degree of comic sophistication, thus rendering the film pleasantly innocuous.

TOPICS FOR DISCUSSION

1. Discuss the supernatural powers of the vampire and the limitations imposed upon the vampire.

2. Trace the gothic elements found in *Dracula*.

3. While at first Renfield seems extraneous to the plot, how does he ultimately serve a definite function?

4. Discuss the peculiar inversion of Christian values found in the novel.

5. Discuss the techniques which Stoker uses to give a sense of verisimilitude to the novel.

6. Discuss the importance of having the vampire be a member of the aristocracy and prey upon refined young ladies rather than upon "ladies of the street."

7. Discuss the various sexual implications found in vampirism – say, for example, seduction through the neck.

8. Discuss the implication that Dracula is merely an evil presence rather than a real character.

SELECTED BIBLIOGRAPHY

BATE, WALTER JACKSON. *From Classic to Romantic*, (1946). A study of the development of gothic fiction.

BAXTER, JOHN. *Hollywood in the Thirties*, (1968).

BENTLEY, C. F. "The Monster in the Bedroom: Sexual Symbolism in Bram Stoker's *Dracula*." *Literature and Psychology*. 22 (1972). Pp. 27-34.

BIRKHEAD, EDITH. *The Tale of Terror*, (1921).

BURKE, EDMUND. *On the Sublime,* (1757). Burke's influential essay emphasized the value of terror and pathos in order to produce a reader's active involvement.

CARTER, HUNTLY. *The Theater of Max Reinhardt,* (1914).

EISNER, LOTTE H. *The Haunted Screen,* (1952, rev. 1965).

FARSON, DANIEL. *The Man Who Wrote* Dracula*: A Biography of Bram Stoker,* (1976).

FLORESCU, RADU AND RAYMOND T. MCNALLY. *Dracula: A Biography of Vlad the Impaler, 1431-1476,* (1973).

LUDLAM, HARRY. *A Biography of Dracula: The Life Story of Bram Stoker,* (1962).

MCNALLY, RAYMOND T. and RADU FLORESCU. *In Search of Dracula: A True History of Dracula and Vampire Legends,* (1972).

PRAZ, MARIO. *The Romantic Agony,* (1933). A study of the history of particular neurotic strains in Romantic literature.

RAILO, EINO. *The Haunted Castle,* (1927). Examines the important motifs of gothic fiction.

SUMMERS, MONTAGUE. *The Gothic Quest,* (1939). An intensive study of the genre up to 1800.

__________. *The Vampire: His Kith and Kin,* (1928).

__________. *The Vampire in Europe,* (1929).

WOLF, LEONARD, ed. *The Annotated Dracula,* (1975). Provides the original text of *Dracula* and includes extensive annotations.

VARMA, P. DAVENDRA. *The Gothic Flame,* (1956). The best recent study.

NOTES

NOTES

NOTES